37 Things One Architect Knows About IT Transformation

A Chief Architect's Journey

Gregor Hohpe

37 Things One Architect Knows About IT Transformation

A Chief Architect's Journey

Gregor Hohpe

Leanpub

Contents

Communication   119

Organizations   173

About this Book

Many large enterprises are facing pressure from the rapid digitalization of the world: "digital disruptors" attack unexpectedly with brand-new business models; the "FaceBook generation" sets dramatically different user expectations; and new technologies have become available in the cloud to everyone with a credit card. This is tough stuff for enterprises that have been, and still are, very successful, but are built around traditional technology and organizational structures. "Turning the tanker", as the need to transform is often described, has become a board room-level topic in most traditional enterprises: "we need new digital products!", "we need to renew our tech stack!", "we need to de-layer our organization!", "we need to become agile!", "we need to become digital!" are the battle cries that often emerge out of the board room. Not as easily done as said.

Senior IT Architects and CTOs play a key role in such a digital transformation endeavor. They combine the technical, communication, and organizational skill to understand how a tech stack refresh can actually benefit the business, what "being agile" and "DevOps" really mean, and which technology infrastructure can improve quality while moving faster. Their job is not an easy one, though: they must maneuver in an organization where IT is often still seen as a cost center, where operations means "run"as opposed to "change", and where middle-aged middle-management has become cozy neither understanding the business strategy nor the underlying technology. It's no surprise then that software / IT architects have become some of the most sought-after IT professionals around the globe.

With such high expectations, though, what does it take to become a successful Chief Architect? And once you get there, how do you get support and keep up? When I became a Chief IT Architect, I wasn't expecting any magic answers, but I was looking for a book that would at least help me not having to reinvent the wheel all the time. I attended many useful CIO/CTO events, but most focused on what the business wanted to achieve and little on how to actually accomplish it on a technical level. Having been unable to find such a book, I decided to collect my experience of over two decades as software engineer, consultant, startup co-founder, and chief architect into a book of my own.

What Things Will I Learn?

The five major sections in this book correspond to the aspects a chief architect has to tackle to effectively support a large IT transformation, starting close to the IT *engine room* and slowly inching up to the organizational *pent house*:

- The role and qualities of an IT architect
- The value of architecture in a large enterprise
- Communicating effectively to a variety of stakeholders
- Understanding organizational structures and systems
- Transforming traditional organizations

You are invited to read this book from beginning to end, following the progression from technical to organizational topics. However, you are just as welcome to peruse the book and start reading whatever peeks your interest. To aid in non-linear navigation, chapters are interlinked through hyperlinks in the e-book version and chapter numbers in parentheses for the print version.

This isn't a technical book. It's a book about how to grow your horizon as an architect to effectively apply your technical skill in large organizations. This book won't teach you how to configure a Hadoop cluster or how to setup container orchestration with Docker and Kubernetes. Instead, it will teach you how to reason about large-scale architectures, how to ensure your architecture benefits the business strategy, how to leverage vendors' expertise, and how to communicate critical decisions to upper management.

Are the Things Proven to Work?

If you are looking for a scientifically proven, repeatable "method" of transforming a technical organization, you may be disappointed. This book's structure is rather loose and you may even be annoyed to have to read through little anecdotes when all you want is the one bit of advice you need in order to be successful. As the title may suggest, this is a personal and somewhat opinionated book: it's based on my daily experiences of two decades in IT, which led me through being a start-up co-founder (lots of fun, not lots of money), system integrator (made tax audits more efficient), consultant (lots of PowerPoint), author (collecting and documenting insights), Internet software engineer (building the future) and chief architect of a large multi-national organization (tough, but rewarding).

I felt that taking a personal account of IT transformation is appropriate because architecture is by nature a somewhat personal business. When looking at a famous building, you can easily identify the architect from afar: white box - Richard Meier, all crooked - Frank Gehry, looks like made from fabric: Zaha Hadid. While not quite as dramatic, every (Chief) IT architect also has his or her personal emphasis and style that's reflected in their works.

The collection of insights that make up this book reflect my personal point of view but are written such that the "nuggets" can be easily extracted and put to broader use. Architects are busy people. I therefore tried to package my insights so that they are easy to consume and even a bit fun to read.

Tell me a Story

I purposefully chose to structure the book as a collection of stories because in our complex world, telling stories is a great way to teach. Studies have shown that people remember stories much better than sheer facts and there appears to be evidence that listening to a story activates additional parts of our brain that help with understanding and retention. Aristotle already knew that a good speech contains not only *logos*, the facts and structure, but also *ethos*, a credible character, and *pathos*, emotions, usually triggered by a good story.

To transform an organization you don't need to solve mathematical equations. You need to move people and that's why you need to be able to tell a good story and paint a compelling vision. It's fine to start out by using some of the attention-catching slogans from this book ("Zombies will eat your brain!") and later supplement them with your own stories. Have you seen people cry and laugh when watching movies, even though they know exactly that the story is fictitious and all acting is fake? That's the power of storytelling in action.

How Come You Know Exactly 37 Things?

The title is a wordplay on O'Reilly's successful books *97 Things Every Software Architect Should Know* and *97 Things Every Programmer Should Know* to both of which I contributed. Seven is a nice digit because it has two syllables and a soft sound. "thirty-eight" sounds harsher than "thirty-seven" and may also remind some people of ammunition. 37 is also a prime number, which is neat. On top of that, 37 is the only two-digit number whose difference between the digits equals the square root of the difference between the number and the least common multiple of its two digits, which surely makes it special! 47 is also a prime number, but doesn't sound as nice and I was pretty certain I don't know 57 things about large-scale IT architecture and transformation, or at least don't have the patience to write that many things down. So there we go with 37 things.

My Urge to Write

Why take the time to write down these articles and anecdotes? Since the Internet became pervasive, writing has taken a slightly different notion for me. When Bobby and I wrote *Enterprise Integration Patterns*, the main purpose was to share our experience with a wide audience. That's still the case with *37 Things*, but inexpensive and abundant on-line storage combined with excellent searchability has brought an additional motivation: to make them more readily available to *myself*, too. I feel that with every written sentence I write, I free up some brain cells to learn new things.

Richard Guindon's famous quote that "Writing is nature's way of telling us how sloppy our thinking is" (see *Writing for Busy People* (17)) also implies that writing well forces you to clean up and sharpen your thoughts. That's exactly what I have done with *37 Things*: a lot of these ideas have been floating in my head for some time. A few started out as informal "ramblings" on my blog[1], others as sketches on a sticky note, and more than a few from a conversation with other architects. Taking the time to write them down, injecting a bit of personal opinion and context here and there, gave me huge satisfaction, and turns a set of random thoughts into a cohesive story.

What's With the Fish?

While animals on the cover of technology books have become a common sight, readers may wonder why I placed a photograph of fish on my cover. It's a combination of consideration and serendipity, really. As this is a fairly personal book that tells stories from my professional career, I wanted to select a personal photo

---

[1]http://www.eaipatterns.com/ramblings

from my travels. The photo of two koi carps swimming upstream in Nagasaki caught my eye because it's dynamic and unique. Swimming upstream is also an apt metaphor for a Silicon Valley veteran transforming corporate IT.

Getting Involved

In the digital age, books needn't be a one-way street. To keep up-to-date, report editorial issues or mistakes, or to discuss the content, please join our discussion group:

> https://groups.google.com/group/37things

Also, feel free to follow me on LinkedIn to see what I am up to:

> http://www.linkedin.com/in/ghohpe

Lastly, while Leanpub is a great platform for publishing incrementally, a book has to be "done" at some point. Naturally, my brain doesn't stop generating new ideas, so those find a home on my Blog:

> https://architectelevator.com/blog

Acknowledgments

Many people have knowingly or unknowingly contributed to this book through hallway conversations, comments in meetings, reviews, or chats over a beer. Perhaps a more humble title would be "37 Things One Architect *Learned*" but perhaps it's not quite as punchy. It's challenging to give due credit to all the people I learned from, but I'd like to highlight Michele Danieli for his constructive feedback, Matthias "Maze" Reik for being a thorough proofreader, Andrew Lee for spotting more typos, my former boss, Barbara Karuth, for reviewing and approving, many of my colleagues insightful conversations, and of course *Kleines Genius* for his untiring support.

1. Fifty Shades of IT

Different Viewpoints of the IT Industry

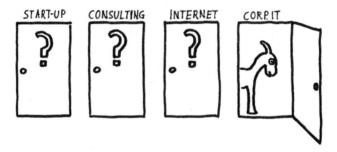

Let's make a deal

When people state that "they are in IT", it can mean many things. They may be working in a business's IT department, may be an independent consultant, work for an enterprise software or hardware vendor, or perhaps be an industry analyst. Other people who deal with *information technology* may not even associate themselves with the term "IT" because it can have negative connotations: many business leaders know IT as a black box where a lot of money goes in and little comes out. At the same time, "IT" is where technology goes to provide business value and runs the world as we know it. I guarantee that you wouldn't want to spend more than a few minutes in a world without corporate IT. That's why I spent a large part of my career in or with IT and find it a fascinating, albeit at times challenging, place.

Navigating the World of IT

I have enjoyed living and working in quite a few cultures around the globe, starting out in Europe, then moving to Silicon Valley before spending almost five years in Tokyo. Perhaps it gave me the drive of an American, the politeness of a Japanese, and the perseverance of a German, or at least a small portion of that desirable target state. Being exposed to a variety of cultures not only brings a diversity of viewpoints, but also humbling experiences like not being able to read signs or maps. Besides experiencing different geographic cultures, "rebooting" a few times into different corporate cultures also provided me with fresh viewpoints and more humbling experiences.

Independent Developer

As a high school and university student I boosted my pocket money as an independent software and hardware developer, developing IBM PC ISA Bus cards for data acquisition and device control – those days computers were big enough to hold scores of extension cards. The corresponding software for chemical chromatography was written in Turbo Pascal aided by 80287 assembly code for numerical analysis. Being able to work from home while doing my studies was great, but most satisfaction came from designing and building a product end-to-end and seeing it live in production. Interestingly, and somewhat unexpectedly, much of those skills came in handy two decades later when designing NFC hardware for Google or automating my home with a Raspberry Pi. It's good to see that some skills remain relevant despite all the technological advances.

Start-up

After completing my studies of computer science in Germany, the German Academic Exchange Service granted me a scholarship for a master's degree at Stanford University. As one does in Silicon Valley, upon graduation I co-founded a startup called Transcape (later renamed to Netpulse) to develop multimedia-enabled exercise equipment. Hiking up Yosemite Valley's Half Dome while the treadmill incline increases with the terrain shown in the video feed was a blast. Gamification elements provided extra motivation, e.g., to deliver pizza in San Francisco by pedaling on an exercise bike. Customers living on top of a hill would place the largest orders, requiring you to pedal extra hard to deliver in time and reap the reward.

Once again combining software and hardware development I learned that all that energy you exert on an exercise bike goes into a simple car alternator connected to a huge resistor. Alas, our founding team had little insight into the health club and exercise machine market. Launching a company during the multimedia wave in the mid-nineties just ahead of the first .com bubble also meant that we had to distribute software and media by shipping CDs. The industry has come a long way in the last 20 years: connectivity, software distribution, mobile user interfaces, and server infrastructure have become trivial. Today you would integrate the exercise machine via Bluetooth to the user's smartphone to deliver an immersive and social experience running in the cloud.

A subsequent short stint at Open Horizons had me building software based on the DCE (Distributed Computing Environment) initiative. Sadly, I couldn't continue due to visa constraints, but it possibly kindled my interest in distributed computing.

IT Consulting

Having enjoyed the start-up spirit, but needing a stable paycheck, I decided to join a system integrator to build large-scale collections and audit systems for the State of California. To be honest, I didn't think that working for the government would be particularly interesting, yet many of my colleagues still remember it as one of

our most exciting projects. Because the government has a mandate
to responsibly manage taxpayer money, they contract systems on
a "benefits basis": vendors only get paid for measurable value delivered, which forced us to deliver value early instead of following
a giant waterfall process with a "big bang" at the end. Pretty agile
for the late nineties.

I valued consulting for the trust the company placed into us as
highly motivated but still pretty young guys to deliver such a
critical and complex system. There were many late-night pizzas
consumed, but also huge successes celebrated. Consulting companies also really understand that people are their biggest asset and
they are willing to invest in their employees with training and
coaching. Of course, it isn't pure altruism – better people translate
into higher billing rates – but in the end all parties win, including
the clients: highly qualified people generally deliver significantly
more value for an only slightly higher price tag.

Being a consultant has distinct advantages. First, once the statement
of work is signed, you are largely immune to the process swamp:
you can use a laptop of your choice, sit anywhere, work in any
department, travel freely, etc. You also won't be in meetings all day
since you are (visibly) too expensive. Lastly, because your career
takes place in the consulting firm's parallel universe, you don't need
to jostle for your own advancement in the organization you are
helping. This affords you important neutrality when shaping the
client's organization.

Strategic "Big 5" Consulting

When I left the system integrator to join a strategic consulting firm,
my boss joked that he'll see me again in 3 months when I will have
gotten fired. I certainly did lack some of the polish (and the attire)
of a management consultant, but the imminent Internet bubble
of 1999/2000 increased the demand for technical staff sufficiently
for me to survive the adjustment process. Among other things, I

learned how to crank PowerPoint like no one else – a skill that came in handy throughout my career. I thoroughly enjoyed working with a variety of clients to bridge the gap between technical details and business strategy. I also learned a lot from the partners, each of whom essentially ran a mini-business.

Working with different vendor products and repeatedly explaining concepts to clients provided the trigger to document design experience in the form of patterns, which ultimately resulted in the book *Enterprise Integration Patterns*[2].

Consultants are often derided as the people who borrow the client's watch to tell them what time it is. Interestingly, most clients who engaged us were either not able to find their watch, agree on which clock to use, read the time, or were stuck in lengthy debates about time zones. The "watch" engagements therefore ended up being some of the most valuable ones for our clients.

Internet Software

Another unlikely transition, triggered mostly by travel fatigue, took me from strategic consulting to Google. Alan Eustace, the VP of engineering at the time, liked to remind us how much he despised the consulting model, which he viewed as people giving smart advice, but not being on the line for delivery and direct impact. Once again, I should consider myself lucky to have slipped in.

Google is an amazing place (as are many other Internet giants): engineers are king, code is king, delivery is king. This is a software business, so delivering running software is what matters. It's not quite the summer camp for developers that many people believe it to be, but rather competitive and disciplined: it's result-driven to the bone and to get funding for a project you first have to prove that you can deliver something fast. The expected ROI is extremely high, but once it's proven (or believed) they are ready to invest. It's a great place to do "IT" for real.

---

[2]http://EnterpriseIntegrationPatterns.com

Corporate IT

Leaving Google to join an insurance company's corporate IT took some courage, but it was equally rewarding to apply the cool technology we built at Google towards a positive impact in a traditional business. It also required me to use both my consulting and technical skills to combine cultural transformation, organizational engineering, and *enterprise architecture* (4).

Insurance isn't known to be a fast mover, but enough changes are coming their way to make them rethink their organizational and IT architecture: connected cars, which are essentially sensors on wheels, enable new pricing models like pay-as-you-drive; the *shareconomy* challenges insurance revenues because it reduces private ownership; the Internet of Things gives an insurance company more data about the "things" it insures, so it can predict and avoid claims before they happen; more frequent and more intense touch points via mobile applications help overcome the challenge that people don't particularly like to talk to their insurance company.

Corporate IT's work environment is decidedly different from a *digital darling*: there's more management, more meetings, more processes, and more friction, often aided by outdated technology (BlackBerry, anyone?). Also, when switching from consulting to a big company, you must remember to apply your achievements towards your internal career as you can't rely on the consulting firm's parallel universe for advancement. This is an easy mistake to make.

Trusted Advisor

After five years turning the tanker, I needed a recharge, and quite honestly the organization also needed time to digest. I therefore returned to Google, assisting customers in their cloud and organizational transformation journey as part of the Office of the CTO.

What's the moral of the story? That I have a difficult time commit-ting? Perhaps, but more importantly it means that I didn't have an interest in doing the same thing under a different label. Instead, I found seeing the different angles of "IT" extremely valuable. Not only does it resemble architectural *viewpoints*, it also highlights each model's strengths and liabilities. I learned how people talk and think differently: Corporate IT *aligns* (26) all the time, consultants "tee off" things and "touch base" without breaking a sweat, while no one at Google ever used buzzwords like "big data", "cloud", or "service-oriented architecture" because all these existed internally before the terms were coined.

It seems one could aspire to innovate like a start-up founder, draw PowerPoints like a management consultant, code like an Internet engineer, and have the political skills of a Corporate IT denizen. I will try.

Architects

Overhead or Corporate Savior?

Architects have an exciting, but sometimes challenging life in corporate IT. Many managers and technical staff consider them overpaid ivory tower residents who, detached from reality, bestow their thoughts upon the rest of the company with slides and wall-sized posters, while their quest for irrelevant ideals causes missed project timelines.

Still, IT architects have become some of the most sought-after IT professionals as traditional enterprises are looking to transform their IT landscape. At the same time, many of the most successful digital companies have a world-class software and systems architecture, but don't have architects at all. So what makes a successful architect?

What Architects Are Not

Sometimes it's easier to describe what something *isn't* rather than trying to come up with an exact definition of what it is. In the case of architects, exaggerated expectations can paint a picture of someone who solves intermittent performance problems in the morning while transforming the enterprise culture in the afternoon. This leads to a scenario where architects are pulled into several roles that clearly miss the purpose of being an architect:

Firefighter - Many managers expect architects to be able to troubleshoot and solve any crisis based on their broad understanding of the current system landscape. An architect shouldn't ignore production issues because they provide valuable feedback into possible architectural weaknesses. But an architect that runs from one fire drill to the next won't have any time to do actual architecture. Architecture requires *thinking*, which cannot be achieved in 30-minute time slots.

Senior Developer - Developers often feel they need to become an architect as the next step in their career (and their pay grade). However, becoming an architect and a superstar engineer are two different career paths, with neither being superior to the other. Architects tend to have a broader scope, including organizational and strategic aspects, whereas engineers tend to specialize and deliver running software. Ideally, the Chief IT Architect in a large organization is good friends with the senior developers.

Project Manager - Architects must be able to juggle many distinct, but interrelated topics. Their decisions also take into account, and impact, project time lines, staffing, and required skill sets. As a result, upper management often comes to rely on the architect for information and decisions regarding the project, especially if the project manager is busy *filling out status report templates* (26). This is a slippery slope for an architect because it's valuable work, but distracts from the architect's main responsibility.

Scientist - While architects need to sport a sharp intellect and must be able to *think in models and systems* (10), an architect's role is to make decisions related to concrete projects and business initiatives. This often separates the role of a *Chief Architect* from that of a *Chief Scientist*, although the lines are blurry – I know a few Chief Scientists who are very hands-on. Personally, I prefer the title *Chief Engineer* to highlight that architects produce more than paper. Lastly, while scientists have a tendency to make things more complex and difficult to understand, an architect's job is to *make complex topics easy to understand* (16).

Measuring an Architect's Value

 Someone once asked me what KPI (Key Performance Indicator) should be used to measure an architect's value. When he suggested the number of decisions made, I was a little stunned and at the same time convinced that this wasn't the right one. Making decisions is important, but *avoiding decisions* (6) can also be a key element of being an architect.

Instead, I suggest two alternative ways to measure value. First, if your systems are still running and can absorb change at a reasonable rate after 5 years, there was likely a good architect involved. For a more concrete description, senior architects in the enterprise work at three levels:

- Define the *IT Strategy*, e.g., by assuring that the IT landscape adequately supports the business strategy or defining a set of necessary IT characteristics for systems to be built or bought. Strategy also includes "retiring" systems (in the *Blade Runner* sense of the word) lest you want to *live among Zombies* (12).
- Exercise *Governance* over the IT landscape to achieve harmonization, complexity reduction, and to make sure that systems integrate into a meaningful whole. Governance occurs through architecture review boards and *inception* (28).
- Deliver *Projects* to stay grounded in reality and receive feedback on decisions from real project implementations. Otherwise *control remains an illusion* (23).

Architects as Change Agents

As the digital economy changes the rules of the game, an architect's role also fundamentally changes. Today's large-scale architects are a critical enabler of IT transformation. To do so, they must be equipped with a special set of skills beyond just technology so that they can...

- ...transcend organizational levels by *riding the architect elevator* (2).
- ...adopt multiple personas which may resemble *movie characters* (3).
- ...*connect business and IT* (4).
- ...bring more than skill as that's just one of the *three legs they stand on* (5).
- ...have *good decision discipline* (6) in face of uncertainty.
- ...*question everything* (7) to get to the root of problems.

2. The Architect Elevator

From the penthouse to the engine room and back

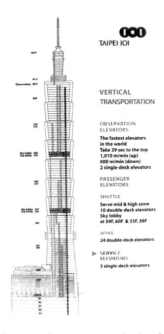

TAIPEI IOI

VERTICAL
TRANSPORTATION

OBSERVATION
ELEVATORS
**The fastest elevators
in the world
Take 39 sec to the top
1,010 m/min (up)
600 m/min (down)
2 single-deck elevators**

PASSENGER
ELEVATORS

SHUTTLE
**Serve mid & high zone
10 double-deck elevators
Sky lobby
at 59F, 60F & 35F, 36F**

OFFICE
24 double-deck elevators

SERVICE
ELEVATORS
3 single-deck elevators

Tall buildings need someone to ride the elevator

A Missing Link

Architects play a critical role as a connecting and translating element, especially in large organizations where departments speak different languages, have different viewpoints, and drive towards

conflicting objectives. Many layers of management only exacer-
bate the problem as communicating up-and-down the corporate
ladder resembles the "telephone game"[3]. The worst case scenario
materializes when people holding relevant information or expertise
aren't empowered to make decisions while the decision makers lack
relevant information. Not a good state to be in for a corporate IT
department, especially in the days where technology has become a
driving factor for most businesses.

The Architect Elevator

Architects can fill an important void in large enterprises: they work
and communicate closely with technical staff on projects, but are
also able to convey technical topics to upper management *without
losing the essence of the message* (16). Conversely, they understand
the company's business strategy and can translate it into technical
decisions that support it.

If you picture the levels of an organization as the floors in a
building, architects can ride what I call the *architect elevator*: they
ride the elevator up and down to move between a large enterprise's
board room and the *engine room* where software is being built. Such
a direct linkage between the levels has become more important than
ever in times of rapid IT evolution and digital disruption.

Stretching the analogy to that of a large ship, if the bridge spots
an obstacle and needs to turn the proverbial tanker, it will set the
engines to reverse and the rudder turned hard to starboard. But if
in reality the engines are running full speed ahead, a major disaster
is preprogrammed. This is why even old steamboats had a pipe to
echo commands directly from the captain to the boiler room and
back. In large enterprises architects have to play exactly that role!

---

[3]In the telephone game children form a circle and relay a message from one child to the
next. When the message returns to the originator they realize that it has completely changed
along the way.

Some Organizations Have More Floors Than Others

Coming back to the building metaphor, the number of floors an architect has to ride in the elevator depends on the type of organization. Flat organizations may not need the elevator at all – a few flights of stairs are sufficient. This may also mean that the up-and-down role of an architect is less critical: if management is keenly aware of the technical reality at the necessary level of detail and technical staff have direct access to senior management, fewer "enterprise" architects are needed. One could say that digital companies live in a bungalow and hence don't need the elevator.

However, classic IT shops in large organizations tend to have many, many floors above them. They live in a skyscraper so tall that a single architect elevator may not be able to span all levels. In this case it's OK if a technical architect and an enterprise architect meet in the middle and cover their respective "half" of the building. The value of the architects in this scenario shouldn't be measured by how "high" they travel, but by how many floors they span. It's a common mistake in large organizations for the folks in the penthouse to only see and value the architects in the upper half of the building. Conversely, many developers or technical architects consider such "enterprise" architects less useful because they don't code. This can be true in some cases – such architects often enjoy life in the upper floors so much that they aren't keen to take the elevator ever down again. But an "enterprise" architect who travels half way down the building to share the strategic vision with technical architects can have a significant value.

Not a One Way Street

Invariably you will meet folks who ride the elevator, but only once to the top and never back down. They enjoy the good view from the penthouse too much and feel that they didn't work so hard to still be visiting the grimy engine room. Frequently you will hear the following comment from these folks: "I used to be technical". I can't help but retort: "I used to be a manager" (it's true) or "Why did you stop? Were you no good at it"? If you want to be more diplomatic (and philosophical) about it, cite Fritz Lang's movie *Metropolis* where the separation between penthouse and engine room almost led to a complete destruction of the city before everyone realized that "the head and the hands need a mediator". In any case: the elevator is meant to be ridden up and down. Eating caviar in the penthouse while the basement is flooded is not the way to transform corporate IT.

Riding the elevator up-and-down is also an important mechanism for the architect to obtain feedback on decisions and to understand their ramifications at the implementation level. Long project implementation cycles don't provide a good *Learning Loop* (32) and can lead to an *Architect's Dream, Developer's Nightmare* scenario. Allowing architects to only enjoy the view from high up, invariably leads to the dreaded authority without responsibility[4] anti-pattern. This pattern can only be broken if architects have to live with, or at least observe, the consequences of their decisions. To do so, they must keep riding the elevator.

High-Speed Elevators

In the past, IT decisions were fairly far removed from the business strategy: IT was pretty "vanilla" and the main parameter (or KPI = Key Performance Indicator) was *cost*. Therefore, riding the elevator wasn't as critical as new information was rare. Nowadays, though, the linkage between business goals and technology choices has become much more direct, even for "traditional" businesses. For example, the desire for faster time to market to meet competitive pressures translates into the need for an elastic cloud approach

---

[4]http://c2.com/cgi/wiki?AuthorityWithoutResponsibility

to computing, which in turn requires applications that scale horizontally and thus should be designed to be stateless. Targeted content on customer channels necessitates analytical models which are tuned by churning through large amounts of data via a Hadoop cluster, which favors local hard drive storage over shared network storage. The fact that in one or two sentences a business need has turned into application or infrastructure design highlights the need for architects to ride the elevator. Increasingly they have to take the express elevator, though, to keep up with the pace at which business and IT are intertwined.

In traditional IT shops, the lower floors of the building can be exclusively occupied by *external consultants* (34), which allows enterprise architects to avoid getting their hands dirty. However, because it focuses solely on efficiency and ignores *Economies of Speed* (31), it's a poor setup in times of rapid technology evolution. Architects who are used to such an environment must stretch their role from being pure consumers of vendors' technology roadmaps to actively defining it. To do so, they must develop their own *IT World View* (13).

Other Passengers

If you are riding the elevator up and down as a successful architect, you may encounter other folks riding with you. You may, for example, meet business or non-technical folks who learned that a deeper understanding of IT is critical to the business. Be kind to those folks, take them with you and show them around. Engage them in a dialog – it will allow you to better understand business needs and goals. They might even take you to the higher floors you haven't been to.

You may also encounter folks who ride the elevator down merely to pick up buzzwords to sell as their own ideas in the penthouse. We don't call these people architects. People who ride the elevator but don't get out are commonly called *lift boys*. They benefit from the ignorance in the penthouse to pursue a "technical" career without touching actual technology. You may be able to convert some of these folks by getting them genuinely interested in what's going on in the engine room. If you don't succeed, it's best to maintain the proverbial elevator silence, avoiding eye contact by examining every ceiling tile in detail. Keep your "elevator pitch" for those moments when you share the cabin with a senior executive, not a mere messenger.

Dangers of Riding the Elevator

You would think that architects riding the elevator up and down are highly appreciated by their employer. After all, they provide significant value to businesses looking to transform their IT to better compete in a digital world. Surprisingly, such architects may encounter unexpected resistance. Both the penthouse and the engine room may have grown quite content with being disconnected: the company leadership is under the false impression that the digital transformation is proceeding well while the folks in the engine room enjoy the freedom to play with any new technology irrespective of its relationship to the business need. Such a situation resembles a cruise ship heading for an iceberg while running the engines full speed ahead. By the time the leadership realizes what's going on, it's likely too late. I sometimes liken such an organization to the Leaning Tower of Pisa where the foundation and the penthouse aren't vertically aligned. Riding the elevator in such a building is certainly more challenging.

When stepping into such an environment, the architect riding the elevator must be prepared to face resistance from both sides. I was once criticized by the "engine room" for pushing corporate agenda against the will of the developers while at the same time corporate leadership chastized me for wanting to try new solutions just for fun. No one ever said being a disruptor is easy, especially as *systems resist change* (10). The best strategy is to start linking the levels carefully and to wait for the right moment to share information. For example, you could help the folks in the engine room explain the great work they are doing to management. Doing so gives them more visibility and recognition while giving you access to detailed technical information.

Other corporate denizens not content with you riding the elevator can be the occupants of the middle floors: they see you whizzing by to connect leadership and the engine room, giving them the feeling of being bypassed. I have called this the "hourglass" curve of appreciation: top management sees you as a critical transformation enabler while the folks in the engine room are happy to have someone to talk to who actually understands and appreciates their work. The folks in the middle see you as a threat to their livelihood, including their children's education and their vacation home in the mountains. This is a delicate affair. Some may actually actively block you on your way: being stopped at every floor to demand an explanation makes riding the elevator not really faster than taking the stairs.

Flattening the Building

Instead of tirelessly riding the elevator up and down, why not get rid of all those unnecessary floors? After all, the digital companies your business is trying to compete with don't have so many floors either. Unfortunately, you can't simply eliminate some floors without blowing the whole building up and being left with a pile of rubble. Eliminating the guys on the middle floors would be a major fallacy anyway because they are often major knowledge holders about the organization and IT landscape, especially if there's a large *black market* (25).

Flattening the building little-by-little may be a sound long-term strategy, but it would take too long because it requires fundamental changes to the company culture. It also changes or eliminates the role played by the folks inhabiting the middle floors, which will put up a fierce resistance. This isn't a fight an architect can win. However, an architect can start to loosen things up a little bit, for example by getting the penthouse interested in information from the engine room, providing faster feedback loops, and reducing the number of PowerPoint status updates given by middle management.

3. Movie Star Architects

An enterprise architect's personas

The architect walk of fame

What should an architect be doing besides riding the elevator? Let's try another analogy: movie characters.

Before the movie starts, you'll get to watch commercials or short films. In our case it's a short film about the origin of the word "architect": it derives from the Greek ἀρχιτέκτων ("architekton"), which roughly translates into "chief builder". Keeping in mind that this word was meant for people who built houses and structures, not IT systems, we should note that the word implies "builder", not "designer" - an architect should be someone who builds, not someone who only draws pretty pictures. An architect is also expected to be accomplished in his or her profession as to deserve the attribute of being a "master". Now to the main feature...

The Matrix - The Master Planner

If you ask tech folk to name a prototypical architect in the movies you are likely to hear *The Matrix* trilogy. The architect of the Matrix is a "cold, humorless, white-haired man in a light gray suit" (Wikipedia[5]), which he largely owes to the fact that he is a computer program himself. Wikipedia also describes that the architect "speaks in long logical chains of reasoning", something that many IT architects are known to do. So perhaps the analogy holds?

The Matrix architect is also the ultimate authority: he designed the Matrix (a computer program to simulate reality to humans being farmed by machines as an energy source) and knows and controls everything. Enterprise architects are sometimes seen as such a person - the all-knowing decision maker. Some even wish themselves into such a role, partly because it is neat to be all-knowing and partly because it gets you a lot of respect. Naturally, this role model has some issues: all-knowingness is a little (too) challenging for humans, meaning we should expect a fair amount of bad decision making and all sorts of other problems. Even if the architect is a super smart person, he or she can base decisions only on those facts that are known to them. In large companies, this inevitably means relying on PowerPoint slides or statements from middle management as it is impossible to be in touch with all technology that is in place, no matter how often you *ride the elevator* (2) down to the engine room. Such an information channel to the supreme decision maker tends to be heavily guarded by people who understand its value as an influencing vehicle, which results in the architect being fed indirect, often biased information. Basing decisions on such a model is dangerous.

In summary: Corporate IT is no movie and its role isn't to provide an illusion for humans being farmed as power sources. We should be cautious with this role model.

---

[5]http://en.wikipedia.org/wiki/Architect_%28The_Matrix%29

Fun fact: Vint Cerf, one of the key architects of the Internet, bears a remarkable resemblance to the Matrix architect. Considering Vint designed much of the Matrix we live in, this may not be a pure coincidence.

Edward Scissorhands - The Gardener

A slightly more fitting analogy for enterprise architects is that of a gardener. I tend to depict this metaphor with a character from one of my favorite movies, *Edward Scissorhands*. Large-scale IT is much like a garden: things evolve and grow on their own with weeds growing the fastest. The role of the gardener is to trim and prune what doesn't fit and to establish an overall balance and harmony in the garden, keeping in mind plants' needs. For example, shade-loving plants should be planted near large trees or bushes. A good gardener is no dictatorial master planner and certainly doesn't make all the detailed decisions about which direction a strain of grass should grow – Japanese gardens being a possible exception. Rather, the gardener sees him or herself as the caretaker of a living ecosystem. Some gardeners, like Edward, are true artists!

I like this analogy as it has a soft touch to it. Complex enterprise IT does feel organic and good architecture has a sense of balance, which can also often be found in a nice garden. Top-down governance with weed killer is unlikely to have a lasting effect and usually does more harm than good. Whether this thinking leads to a new application for *The Nature of Order*[6], I am not sure yet. I should go read it.

Vanishing Point - The Guide

Erik Dörnenburg, ThoughtWorks' Head of Technology Europe, introduced me to another very apt metaphor. Erik closely works with

---

[6]Alexander: The Nature of Order, Center for Environmental Structure, 2002

many software projects, which tend to loathe the ostensibly all-knowing, all-decision-making architect who is disconnected from reality. Erik even coined the term *architecture without architects*, which might cause some architects to worry about their career.

Erik likens an architect to a tour guide, someone who has been to a certain place many times, can tell a good story about it, and can gently guide you to pay attention to important aspects and avoid unnecessary risks. This is a guiding role: tour guides cannot force their guests to follow their advice, except maybe those who drop off a bus load of tourists at a tourist trap restaurant in the middle of nowhere.

This type of architect has to "lead by influence" and has to be hands-on enough to earn the respect of those he or she is leading. The tour guide also stays along for the ride and doesn't just hand a map to the tourists like some consultant architects are known to do. An architect who acts as a guide often depends on strong management support because evidence that good things happened due to his or her guidance may be subtle. In purely "business case-driven" environments this could be limiting the "tour guide" architect's impact or career.

An unconventional guide out of another one of my favorite movies is the blind DJ *Super Soul* from the 1971 road movie *Vanishing Point*. Like so may IT projects the movie's protagonist, Kowalski, is on a death march with an impossible deadline to meet and numerous obstacles along the way. He isn't delivering code, but a 1970 Dodge Challenger R/T 440 Magnum from Denver to San Francisco - in 15 hours. Kowalski is being guided by Super Soul who has tapped the police network, just like architects plugging into the management network, to get access to crucial information. The guide tracks Kowalski's progress and keeps the hero clear of all sorts of traps that police (i.e., management) has setup. After Super Soul is compromised by "management", the "project" gets adrift and ends like too many IT projects: in a fiery crash.

The Wizard of Oz

Architects can sometimes be seen as wizards that can solve just about any technical challenge. While that can be a short-term ego boost, it's not a good job description and expectation to live up to. Hence by the "wizard" architect analogy I don't mean an actual wizard waving the magic wand, but the "Mighty Oz" - a video projection that appears large and powerful, but is in fact controlled by a mere human "wizard", who turns out to be an ordinary man who uses the big machinery to garner respect.

A gentle dose of such engineered deception can be of use in large organizations where "normal" developers are rarely involved in management discussions or major decisions. This is where the "architect" title can be used to make oneself a bit more "great and mighty": the projection can garner the respect of the general population and can even be a precondition to taking the elevator to the top floors. Is this cheating? I would say "no" as long as you don't get enamored in so much wizardry that you forget about your technical roots.

Superhero? Superglue!

Similar to the wizard, another expectation of the architect is that of the superhero: if you believe some job postings, enterprise architects can single-handedly catapult companies into the digital age, solve just about any technical problem, and are always up-to-date on the latest technology. These are tough expectations to fulfill, so I'd caution any architect against taking advantage of this common misconception.

Amir Shenhav from Intel appropriately pointed out that instead of the superhero we need "super glue" architects - the guys who hold architecture, technical details, business needs, and people together across a large organization or complex projects. I like this metaphor as it resembles the analogy of an architect being a catalyst. We just have to be a little careful: being the glue (or catalyst) means understanding a good bit about the things you glue together. We don't talk about the architect as a pure matchmaker.

Making the Call

Which type of architect should one be? First, there are likely many more types and movie analogies. You could play "Inception" and create architectural dream worlds with a (dangerous) twist. Or be one of the two impostors debating Chilean architecture in "There's Something about Mary" or (more creepily) Anthony Royal in the utopian drama "High-rise" - the opportunities are manifold.

In the end, most architects exhibit a combination of these proto-typical stereotypes. Periodic gluing, gardening, guiding, impressing and a little bit of all-knowing every now-and-then can make for a pretty good architect.

4. Enterprise Architect or Architect in the Enterprise?

The upper and lower floors of the ivory tower

Architecture from the ivory tower

When I was hired as enterprise architect, *Head of Enterprise Architecture* to be more precise, I had little idea what *enterprise architecture* really entails. I also wondered whether my team should be called *Feet of Enterprise Architecture*, but that contemplation didn't find much love. The driver behind the tendency to prefix titles with "Head of" was aptly described in an on-line forum I stumbled upon:

This title typically implies that the candidate wanted a

director/VP/executive title but the organization refused to extend the title. By using this obfuscation, the candidate appears senior to external parties but without offending internal constituencies.[7]

I am not particularly fond of the "Head of XYZ" title because it focuses on the person heading (no pun intended) a team rather than accomplishing a specific function. I rather name the person by what they need to achieve, assuming that they don't do this alone but have a team supporting them. Luckily, I am now a "Chief" and no longer a "Head", which leaves room, though, for not-quite-politically-correct analogies, which I occasionally stoke by greeting people with a "howgh".

All title prefixes aside, when IT folk meet an *Enterprise Architect*, their initial reaction is to place this person *high up into the penthouse* (2), where they draw pretty pictures that bear little resemblance to reality. To receive a warmer welcome from IT staff, one should therefore be careful with the label *enterprise architect*. However, what is an architect who works at enterprise scale supposed to be called then?

Enterprise Architecture

The recurring challenge with the word "Enterprise Architect" tends to be that it could describe a person that architects the enterprise as a whole (including the business strategy level) or someone doing IT architecture at enterprise level (as opposed to a departmental architect, for example).

To help resolve this ambiguity, let's defer to the defining book on the topic, Jeanne Ross' and Peter Weill's *Enterprise Architecture as Strategy*[8]. Here we learn that

---

[7]https://www.quora.com/What-does-Head-usually-mean-in-job-titles-like-Head-of-Social-Head-of-Product-Head-of-Sales-etc.

[8]Ross, Weill: Enterprise Architecture as Strategy. Harvard Business School Press, 2006

Enterprise architecture is the organizing logic for business processes and IT infrastructure reflecting the integration and standardization requirements of the company's operating model.

Following this definition, *enterprise architecture* (EA) isn't a pure IT function but also considers business processes, which are part of a company's operating model. In fact, the book's most widely publicized diagram[9] shows four quadrants depicting business operating models with higher or lower levels of process standardization (uniformity across lines of business) and process integration (sharing of data and interconnection of processes). Giving industry examples for all quadrants, Ross and Weill map each model to a suitable high-level IT architecture strategy. For example, a data and process integration program may yield little value if the business operating model is one of highly diversified business units with few shared customers. For such enterprises, IT should instead provide a common infrastructure, on top of which each division can implement its diverse processes. Conversely, a business that's composed of largely identical units, such as a franchise, benefits from a highly standardized application landscape. The matrix demonstrates perfectly how enterprise architecture forges the connection between the business and IT. Only if the two are well aligned does IT provide value to the business.

Connecting Business and IT

Connecting business and IT is easier if the business side of the organization also has a well-defined architecture. Luckily, as business environments become more complex and digital disruptors force traditional enterprises to evolve their business models more rapidly, the notion of *Business Architecture* has gained significant attention in recent years. Business architecture translates the *structured,*

---

[9]http://cisr.mit.edu/research/research-overview/classic-topics/enterprise-architecture/

architectural way of thinking (9) that's guided by a formalized view of components and interrelationships, into the business domain. Rather than connecting technical system components and reasoning about technical system properties such as security and scalability, business architecture describes the "the structure of the enterprise in terms if its governance structure, business processes and business information"[10].

The business architecture essentially defines the company operating model, i.e. by defining how business areas are structured and integrated, derived from the business strategy. Meanwhile, the IT architecture builds the corresponding IT capabilities. If the two work seamlessly side-by-side, you don't need much else. If the two aren't well connected, you need something to pull the two together. My proposed definition of enterprise architecture therefore is:

> *Enterprise Architecture is the glue between Business and IT Architecture.*

This definition clarifies that enterprise architecture, unlike IT architecture at enterprise level, isn't an IT function. Accordingly, the EA team should be positioned close to the company leadership and not deep inside the IT organization.

IT is from Mars, Business is from Venus

A strict separation between IT and business that is commonly found in enterprises seems troublesome to me. I tend to jest that in the old days, when everything was running on paper instead of computers, companies also didn't have a separate "paper" department and a CPO - the Chief Paper Officer. In digital companies business and IT are inseparable - IT is the business and the business is IT. Connecting the two gives enterprise architecture a whole new relevance, but also new challenges. It's like adding a mid-floor

---

[10]http://www.omg.org/bawg/

elevator that connects the business folks in the penthouse with the IT folks in the engine room because the respective elevators don't quite reach each other. While highly valuable, in the long run such an EA department's objective must be to make itself obsolete, or at least smaller, by extending the respective elevators. But no worries, rapid changes in both the business and technical environment make it unlikely that the need for EA disappears altogether.

Building a fruitful connection between business and IT architecture is easier if the business architecture is at a comparable level of maturity as IT Architecture, which can present a challenge because business architecture is even less mature as a domain than IT architecture. That's not because businesses had no architecture, but rather because the folks doing business architecture were not identified as such, but were the business leaders, division heads, or COOs. Also, designing the business was rather attributed to business acumen than structured thinking. Where the business produced architecture-like artifacts, they often ended up being "functional capability maps" that *don't include any lines* (22).

Supporting the business is the ultimate goal and *raison d'etre* of all enterprise functions. Positioning IT architecture on par with business architecture highlights, though, that the days where IT was a simple order-taker who provides a commodity resource at the lowest possible cost are (luckily) over. In the digital age, IT is a competitive differentiator and opportunity driver, not a commodity like electricity. The view that Google/Facebook/Amazon etc. "are technology companies while we are an XYZ business" no longer holds: the digital giants are regular businesses - they sell advertising or provide fulfillment of goods. They have simply learned how to use technology for competitive advantage and have shown how powerful that insight is.

The new role of IT has to be reflected in the setup of the architecture function: business drives IT, but IT can also drive new business, and enterprise architecture plays a critical role as the bidirectional interface. Interestingly, this translation between business needs and

IT architecture remains a domain that's perennially short of talent. It appears that folks find comfort on one or the other side of the fence but only a few can, and choose to, credibly play in both worlds. It also means it's a good time to be an enterprise architect.

Architects in the Enterprise

My definition above also implies that some IT architects, who aren't enterprise architects, work at enterprise scope. These are largely the folks I speak about in this book. Because they are the technical folks who have learned to *ride the elevator* (2) to the upper floors to engage with management and business architects, they are a critical element in any IT transformation.

How is being an "enterprise-scale architect" different from a "normal" IT architect? First, everything is bigger. Many large enterprises are conglomerates of different business units and divisions, each of which can be a multi-Billion Dollar business and can be engaged in a different business model. As things get bigger, you will also find more legacy: businesses grow over time or through acquisitions, both of which breed legacy. This legacy isn't constrained to systems, but also to people's mindset and ways of working. Enterprise-scale architects must therefore be able to *navigate organizations* (30) and complex political situations.

Fools with Tools

The scale and complexity of doing architecture at the enterprise level is what makes large-scale IT architecture exciting, but it also presents one of the biggest dangers. It's far too easy to get lost in this complexity and have an interesting time exploring it, without ever producing tangible results. Such cases are the source of the stereotype that enterprise architecture resides in the ivory tower and delivers little value.

Another danger lies in the long feedback cycles. Judging whether someone performs good enterprise architecture takes even longer than judging good IT architecture. While the digital world forces shorter cycles, many enterprise architecture plans still span three to five years. Thus, enterprise architecture can become a hiding ground for wanna-be cartographers. That's why enterprise architects need to *show impact* (5).

Some enterprise architects associate themselves closely with a specific enterprise architecture tool, which captures the diverse aspects of the enterprise landscape. These tools allow structured mapping from business processes and capabilities, ideally produced by the business architects, to IT assets such as applications and servers. Done well, such tools can be the structured repository that builds the bridge between business and IT architecture. Done poorly, they become a never-ending discovery and documentation process that produces a deliverable that's *missing an emphasis* (18) and is outdated by the time it's published.

Visit all Floors

Architecture, if taken seriously, provides significant value at all levels. The short film *Powers of 10*, produced in 1977 by Charles and Ray Eames for IBM, comes to mind: the film zooms out from a picnic in Chicago by one order or magnitude every ten seconds until it reaches 10^{24}, showing a sea of galaxies. Subsequently, it zooms in until at 10^{-18} it shows the realm of *quarks*. Interestingly, the two views don't look all that different. I feel that large enterprises are the same: the complexity seems similar from far out as it's from up close. It's almost like a fractal structure: the more you zoom in or out, the more it looks the same. Therefore, performing serious enterprise architecture is as complex and as valuable as fixing a Java concurrency bug, as long as the enterprise architects leave the ivory tower penthouse and take the elevator at least a few floors down.

5. An Architect Stands on Three Legs

Architects need to scale horizontally

A three-legged stool does not wobble

What does an IT Architect do? Well, IT Architects are the people who make IT architecture. This leaves us with having to define *what architecture is* (9). Assume, we managed this task, what does a good architect become after many successful years? Take up residence in the *penthouse* (2)? Hopefully not. Become a CTO? Not a bad choice. Or remain a (senior) architect? That's what famous building architects do. Then, however, we need to understand what distinguishes a senior IT architect from a junior one.

Skill, Impact, Leadership

When asked to characterize the seniority of an architect, I resort to a simple framework that I believe applies to most high-end professions. A successful architect has to stand on 3 "legs":

1. *Skill* is the foundation for practicing architects. It requires knowledge and the ability to apply the knowledge.
2. *Impact* measures how well an architect applies his or her skill in projects to the benefit of a project or a company.
3. Lastly, *leadership* assures that the state of the practice advances and more architects are grown.

This classification maps well to other professional fields such as medicine: after studying and acquiring skill, doctors practice and treat patients before they go to publish in medical journals and pass their learnings to the next generation of doctors.

Skill

Skill is the ability to apply relevant knowledge, for example about specific technologies, such as Docker, or architectures, such as Cloud Architectures. Knowledge can usually be acquired by taking a course, reading a book, or perusing on-line material. Most (but not all) certifications focus on verifying knowledge, partly because it's easily mapped to a set of multiple choice questions. Knowledge is like having a drawer chest full of tools. Skill implies knowing when to open which drawer and which tool to use.

Impact

Impact is measured in benefit for the business, usually in additional revenue or reduced cost. Faster times to market or the ability to incorporate unforeseen requirements late in the product cycle without having to start over positively affect revenue and therefore count as impact. Focusing on impact is a good exercise for architects to not drift off into PowerPoint-land. As I converse with colleagues about what distinguishes a great architect, we often identify *rational and disciplined decision-making* (6) as a key factor in translating skill into impact. This doesn't mean that just being a good decision maker makes a good architect. You still need to know your stuff.

Leadership

Leadership acknowledges that experienced architects do more than make architecture. For example, they should mentor junior architects by passing on their knowledge and experience. They should also further the state of the field as a whole, for example through publications, teaching, speaking engagements, research or blogging.

The Virtuous Cycle

While the model is rather simple, just as a stool cannot stand on two legs it's important to appreciate the balance between the three aspects. Skill without impact is where new architects start out as students or apprentices. But soon it is time to get out into the world and make an impact. Architects that don't make an impact don't have a place in a for-profit business.

Impact without leadership is a typical place for a solution architect who is engrained in projects. However, without leadership this architect will hit a glass ceiling and won't become a thought leader in the field. Many companies don't put enough emphasis on nurturing or pushing their architects to this level out of fear that any distraction from daily project work will cost them money. As a result, architects in these companies plateau at an intermediate level and typically won't lead the company to innovative or transformative solutions. Missing such opportunities is penny-wise and pound-foolish. In contrast, some companies like IBM formalize the aspect of leadership as "give back": distinguished engineers and fellows are expected to give back to the community inside and outside the company.

Likewise, leadership without (prior) impact lacks foundation and may be a warning signal that you have become an ivory tower architect with a weak relation to reality. This undesirable effect can also happen when the impact stage of an architect lies many years or even decades back: the architect may preach methods or insights that are no longer applicable to current technologies. While some insights are timeless, others age with technology: putting as much logic as possible into the database as stored procedures because it speeds up processing is no longer a wise approach as the database turns out to be the bottleneck in most modern web-scale architectures. The same is true for architectures that rely on nightly batch cycles. Modern 24/7 real-time processing doesn't have any night.

The circle closes when a senior architect mentors junior architects. Because feedback cycles in (software) architecture are inherently slow, this process can save new architects many years of learning by doing and making mistakes. 10 well-mentored junior architects will have more impact than one senior architect. Every architect should know that scaling vertically (getting smarter) only works up to a certain level and can imply a single point of failure (you!). Therefore, you need to scale horizontally by deploying your knowledge to multiple architects. As I am continuously trying to recruit architects and sense that many other large enterprises are in a similar need of architects, scaling the skill set is as important as ever.

Mentoring not only benefits the mentee, but also the mentor. The old saying that to really understand something you need to teach it to someone else is most true for architecture. Likewise, giving a talk or *writing a paper* (16) requires you to sharpen your thoughts, which often leads to renewed insight.

You spin me right round…

Experienced architects will correctly interpret the 1980s reference to mean that an architect doesn't complete the virtuous cycle just once. This is partly driven by ever changing technologies and architectural styles. While a person may already be a thought leader in relational databases, he or she may need to acquire new skill in NoSQL databases. The second time around acquiring skill is usually significantly faster because you can build on what you already know. After a sufficient number of cycles we may in fact experience what the curmudgeons always knew: that there is really not much new in software architecture and that we've seen it all before.

Another reason to repeat the cycle is that the second time around our understanding may be at a much deeper level. The first time around we may have learned how to do things, but only the second time we may understand *why*. For example, it's likely no misrepresentation that writing *Enterprise Integration Patterns* is a form of thought leadership. Still, some of the elements such as the pattern icons or the decision trees and tables in the chapter introductions were more accidental than based on deep insight. Only now in hindsight we understood them as instances of a visual pattern language or pattern-aided decision approaches. Thus it's often worthwhile to make another cycle.

Architect as terminal stage?

While architects have one of the most exciting jobs, some people may be sad to see that being an architect implies that you'll likely remain one for most of your career. I am not so worried about that. First, this puts you in a good peer group of CEOs, presidents, doctors, lawyers, and other high-end professionals. Second, in technically minded organizations, software engineers should feel the same: your next career step should be to become a senior software engineer or *staff engineer*. The goal is, therefore, to detach the job title of *software engineer* or *IT architect* from a specific seniority level. At many digital organizations the software engineer career ladder reaches all the way to SVP (Senior Vice President) level with commensurate standing and compensation. Some organizations even know a *chief engineer*, which, if you think about it, may be a better title than chief architect. Personally, I prefer to get better at what I like doing than trying to chase something else. Keep architecting!

6. Making Decisions

Sometimes you decide not to decide

(IT) Life is full of choices

You buy a lottery ticket and win. What a fantastic decision! You cross the road at night, on red, on a busy street, drunk, and with your eyes closed. You arrive safely on the other side. Also a good decision? Doesn't sound like it. But what's the difference? Both decisions had positive outcomes. In the latter case, though, we judge by the risk involved while in the former we focus on the outcome, ignoring the ticket price and the odds of winning. However, you can't judge a decision by the outcome alone, simply because you didn't know the outcome when you made the decision.

Another exercise: in front of you is a very large jar. It contains 1,000,000 pills. They all look the same, are all tasteless and benign, except one, which will kill you instantly and painlessly. How much money does someone have to pay you to take a pill from this jar? Most people will answer 1 million Dollars, 10 million Dollars, or straight-out refuse. However, the same people are quite willing to cross the road on a red light (with their eyes open), which carries the same risk as swallowing a couple of pills. It'd be difficult to argue that the 30 seconds you saved by crossing on red would have earned you the equivalent of a few million Dollars.

Humans are actually terrible decisions makers, especially when small probabilities and grave outcomes like death are involved. Kahneman's book *Thinking, Fast and Slow*[11] shows so many examples of how our brain can be tricked, it can make you wonder how humanity could get this far despite being such terrible decision makers. I guess we had a lot of tries.

Making decisions is a critical part of an enterprise-scale architect's job and many IT decisions, for example, cybersecurity risks or system uptime have similar characteristics of small probability but grave downsides. Being a good architect therefore warrants a conscious effort to becoming a better decision-maker.

The Law of Small Numbers

Contrived examples make erratic or illogical behavior quite apparent. But when faced with complex business decisions, poor decision-making discipline often isn't as obvious.

 I attended weekly operations meetings that labeled weeks "good" or "bad" based on the number of critical infrastructure outages. I relabeled those weeks as "lucky" because lowering the number and severity of incidents in the long run is the real metric to observe.

---

[11]Kahneman, Daniel: Thinking, Fast and Slow, Farrar, Straus and Giroux; 2013

Such thinking is the corporate IT equivalent of "after 5 times black it's gotta be red!" My shocker version of highlighting such flawed thinking consists of a (fictitious) sequence of events during Russian Roulette: "click – I am a genius! – boom". Kahneman calls this "The law of small numbers" – people tend to jump to conclusions based on sample sizes that are way too small to be significant. For example, zero outages in a week are no cause for celebration in a large enterprise.

 Google's mobile ads team used rigid metrics for A/B testing experiments that affected ad appearance or selection. The dashboard included metrics like click-through rates (more clicks = more money), but also indicate if ads distract from the search results (Google.com is a search engine, not an ads engine). Each metric showed a confidence interval, which represents the range that 95% of sample sets would randomly fall into. If your experiment's improvement landed inside the confidence interval, you'd have to extend the experiment to get valid data (for normal distributions, the confidence interval narrows with the square root of the number of sample points).

IT purchasing decisions are often made based on extensive require-ment lists that are calculated into scores. However, when you pick the "winner" with a score of 82.1 over the "loser" with 79.8, it'd be challenging to prove the statistic significance of this decision. Still, numeric scores may be better than *traffic light* comparison tables that rate each attribute as "green", "yellow", or "red". A product may get "green" for allowing time travel, but a "red" for requiring planned downtime. While this may make it look roughly equivalent to one with the opposite properties, I know which one I'd prefer. Sadly, such comparison charts are often either reverse-engineered from a preferred outcome or the desire to maintain the status quo. I have seen IT requirements analogous to demanding that a new car must rattle at 60 mph and have a squeaky door in order to appropriately replace the existing one.

Bias

Kahneman's book lists so many ways in which our thinking is biased that it's really worth reading. For example, *confirmation bias* describes our tendency to interpret data in such a way that it supports our own hypotheses. The Google Ad dashboard was designed to overcome this bias.

Another well-known bias is *prospect theory*: when faced with an opportunity, people tend to favor a smaller, but guaranteed gain over the uncertain chance for a larger one – "A sparrow in the hand is better than the pigeon on the roof." When it comes to taking a loss, however, people are likely to take a (long) shot at avoiding the penalty over coughing up a smaller amount for sure. We tend to "feel lucky" when we can hope to escape a negative event, an effect called *loss aversion*. Studies show that people typically demand 1.5 to 2 times the rational payoff to take a gamble on a positive outcome. Being offered a coin toss that makes them pay $100 on head but gives them $120 on tail, most people will kindly decline despite the expected value being 0.5 x -$100 + 0.5 x $120 = $10. Most people will accept the offer when the payout is between $150 and $200.

 I am sure you have seen project managers avoid the certain loss in velocity for performing a major refactoring because the payoff in system stability or sustained velocity is uncertain. They are feeling lucky.

Priming

Another phenomenon, *priming*, can influence decisions based on recent data we received. In the extreme case, when faced with enormous uncertainty, it can make us pick a number we recently heard or saw even if it's totally unrelated. This effect plays a role when many people answer 1 million Dollars when faced with the 1 million pills example.

Priming is routinely used in retail scenarios. When you go to buy a piece of clothing, let's say a sweater, the store clerk is almost guaranteed to first show you something expensive, even outside your price range. A sweater for $399? It's made from cashmere and feels very soft and comfortable; tempting, but it's simply too expensive. But the almost-as-nice sweater for $199 seems a reasonable compromise and you'll happily buy it. Next door, decent sweaters can be had for $59. You fell victim to priming, setting a context that influences your decision. Priming can even make you walk more slowly if your mindset is on elderly people[12].

William Poundstone's book *The Myth of Fair Value*[13] shows that products that no one actually buys can shift purchasing behavior significantly, thanks to priming. When presented with a choice between a "premium" beer for $2.60 and a "bargain" one for $1.80, about two thirds of test subjects (students) chose the premium beer. Adding a third, "super-premium" beer for a whopping $3.40 shifted student's desire so that 90% ordered the premium beer and 10% the super-premium.

Decision Analysis

If we are such horrible decision makers, what can we do to get better at it? Understanding these mechanisms can help you avoid or at least compensate for them. A fantastic book on the mathematics of decision making is Ron Howard's and Ali Abbas' *Foundations of Decision Analysis* [14]. Ron's class was one of the best I took at

---

[12]Bargh, Chen, Burrows: Automaticity of social behavior: Direct effects of trait construct and stereotype activation on action. Journal of Personality and Social Psychology, Vol 71(2), Aug 1996, 230-244.

[13]Poundstone, William: Priceless: The Myth of Fair Value, Hill and Wang, 2011

[14]Howard, Abbas: Foundations of Decision Analysis, Prentice Hall, 2015

Stanford: entertaining, thoughtful, and challenging. His book isn't cheap, though, listing at almost $200. Should you buy a book for $200 that could make you a better decision maker? Think about it...

Micromort

Ron and Ali help us think rationally about the jar with pills from above. A one in one million chance of dying is called 1 *micromort.* Taking one pill from the jar amounts to being exposed to exactly one micromort. The amount you are willing to pay to avoid this risk is called your *micromort value.* Micromorts help us reason about decisions with small probabilities, but very serious outcomes, such as deciding whether to undergo surgery that eliminates lifelong pain, but fails with a 1% probability, resulting in immediate death.

To calibrate the micromort value, it helps to consider the risks of daily life: a day of skiing clocks in at between 1 and 9 micromorts while motor vehicle accidents amount to about 0.5 per day. So a ski trip may run you some 5 micromorts – the same as swallowing 5 pills. Is it worth it? You'd have to compare the enjoyment value you derive from skiing against the trip's cash expense plus the "cost" of the micromort risk you are taking.

So how much should you demand to take one pill? Most people's micromort value lies between $1 and $20. Assuming a prototypical value of $10, the ski trip that may cost you $100 in gas and lift tickets, costs you an extra $50 in risk of death. You should therefore decide whether a day in the mountains is worth $150 to you. This also shows why a micromort value of $1,000,000 makes little sense: You'd hardly be willing to pay $5,000,100 for a one-day ski trip unless you are filthy rich! Lastly, the model helps you judge whether buying a helmet for $100 is a worthwhile investment for you if it reduces the risk of death in half.

The micromort value goes up with income (or rather, consumption) and goes down with age. This is to be expected as the monetary value you assign to your remaining life increases with your income.

A wealthy person should easily decide to buy a $100 helmet while a person who is struggling to make ends meet is more likely to accept the risk. As you age, the likelihood of death from natural causes unstoppably increases until it reaches about 100,000 micromorts annually, or almost 300 per day, by the age of 80. At that point, the value derived from buying a risk reduction of 2 micromorts is rather small.

Model Thinking

Decision models can go a long way in making us better decision makers. Thanks to George Box, it's well-known that "all models are wrong, but some are useful." So don't dismiss a model just because it makes simplifying assumptions. It's likely to help you make a much better decision than your gut. The best overview of models and their application I have come across is Prof. Scott Page's Coursera course on Model Thinking[15]. He also recently published the content in his book *The Model Thinker* [16].

Decision trees are very simple models that make decisions more rational. Let's say you want to buy a car, but there's a 40% chance the dealer will offer a $1000 cash-back starting next month. You need a car now, so if you defer the purchase, you'll need to rent a car for $500 for the coming month, even if the rebate doesn't come through. What should you do? If you buy now, you'll pay the list price, which we calibrate to $0 for simplicity's sake. If you rent first, you are down by $500 with a 40% chance to gain $1000, so the expected value is 0.4 x $1000 − $500 = -$100, lower than the list price. You should buy the car now.

An insider offers to tell you whether the cashback promotion happens next month or not. He asks $150 for this information. Should you buy it? Having this information, your decision tree would allow you to buy now if there's no cashback (in 60% of

[15]https://www.coursera.org/course/modelthinking
[16]Page, Scott E.: The Model Thinker, Basic Books, 2018

cases) and to buy later if there is (in 40% of the cases). That yields an expected value of 0.6 x 0 + 0.4 x (1000 − 500) = $200. As your current best scenario, i.e. buying now, yielded a value of $0, it's worth paying $150 for the extra information.

How do you know that the chance of the cashback is exactly 40%? You don't. But using the model helps you reason in face of uncertainty. You can re-run the model for a 50% likelihood and see whether your decision changes.

Avoiding Decisions

With all this science behind decision making, what's the best decision? It's the one you don't have to take! That's why Martin Fowler observes that "one of an architect's most important tasks is to eliminate irreversibility in software designs"[17]. Those are the decisions that don't need to be made or can be made quickly because they can be easily changed later. In a well-designed software system, decisions aren't as final as when taking deadly pills from a jar.

---

[17]Fowler: Who needs an architect?, http://martinfowler.com/ieeeSoftware/whoNeedsArchitect.pdf

7. Question Everything

Wer nicht fragt, bleibt dumm!

The architect riddler

It's a common misconception that chief architects know everything better than "normal" architects – why else would they be the "chief"? Such thinking is actually pretty far from the truth. Hence I often introduce myself as a person who knows the right questions to ask. Wrangling one more reference from the movie *The Matrix*, visiting the chief architect is a bit like visiting the Oracle: you won't get a straight answer but you will hear what you need to hear.

Five Whys

Asking questions isn't a new technique and has been widely publicized in the "5 whys" approach devised by Sakichi Toyoda as part of the Toyota Production System. It's a technique to get to the root cause of an issue by repeatedly asking why something happened. If your car doesn't start, you should keep asking "why" to find out the starter doesn't turn because the battery is dead because you left the lights on because the beeper that warns you of parking with your lights on didn't sound because of an electronics problem. So instead of just jump-starting the car you should fix the electronics to keep the problem from happening again. In Japanese the method is called "naze-naze-bunseki" (なぜなぜ分析), which roughly translates into "why, why analysis". I therefore consider the number 5 a guideline to not give up too early. I also don't think that you cheated if you identified the actual root cause with just four "whys".

The technique can be quite useful, but requires discipline because people can be tempted to inject their own preferred solutions or assumptions into their answers. I have seen people conducting root-cause analysis on production outages repeatedly answer the second or third question with "because we don't have sufficient monitoring" and the next one with "because we don't have enough budget". The equivalent answer from the car example would be "because the car is old". That's not root cause analysis but opportunism or *excuse-ism*, a word that made it into Urban Dictionary[18], but not yet into Merriam-Webster.

Repeatedly asking questions can annoy people a slight bit, so it's good to have the reference to the Toyota Production System handy to highlight that it's a widely adopted and useful technique instead of you just being difficult. It's also helpful to remind your counterparts that you are not challenging their work or competence, but that your job requires you to understand systems and problems in detail so you can spot potential gaps or misalignments.

---

[18]http://urbandictionary.com

Whys Reveal Decisions and Assumptions

When conducting architecture reviews, "why" is a useful question as it helps draw attention to the *Decisions* (9) that were made as well as the assumptions and principles that led to those decisions. Too often results are presented as "god-given" facts that "fell from the sky" or wherever you believe the all-deciding divine creator (the real chief architect!) resides. Uncovering the assumptions that led to a decision can provide much insight and increase the value of an architecture review. An architecture review is not only looking to validate the results, but also the thinking and decisions behind. To emphasize this fact one should request an Architecture Decision Record[19] from any team submitting an architecture for review.

Unstated assumptions can be the root of much evil if the environment has changed since the assumptions were made. For example, traditional IT shops often write elaborate GUI configuration tools that could be replaced with a few lines of code and a standard software development tool chain. Their decisions are based on the assumption that writing code is slow and error prone, which no longer holds universally true as we learn once we overcome our *Fear of Code* (11). If you want to change the behavior of the organization, you often have to identify and overcome outdated assumptions first.

Coming back to *The Matrix*, the explanation given by the Oracle that "...you didn't come here to make the choice, you've already made it. You're here to try to understand *why* you made it." could make a somewhat dramatic, but very appropriate opening to an architecture review.

A Workshop for Every Question

A clear and present danger of asking questions in large organizations lies in the fact that people often don't know, can't express, or

---

[19]http://thinkrelevance.com/blog/2011/11/15/documenting-architecture-decisions

are unwilling to give the answer. Their counter-proposal is usually to hold a meeting, most likely a very long one, which is labeled as "workshop", with the purported goal of sharing and documenting the answer. In the actual workshop, though, it frequently turns out that the answer is unknown, leaving you with the job of answering your own questions. The team might also bring external support to defend against you asking too many undesired questions.

Soon your calendar will be full of workshop invitations, allowing teams to blame you for being the bottleneck that slows their progress because you aren't available for their important meetings. And they aren't even lying! Such organizational behavior is an example of *Systems Resisting Change* (10).

If your goal is to not just review architecture proposals, but also to change the behavior of the organization, you have to take up this challenge and change the system. For example, you can re-define the expectations for architecture documentation and obtain management buy-in for doing so, e.g. to increase transparency. If satisfactory documentation isn't produced before the meeting, the workshop must be canceled. If teams are unable to produce such documentation, you can offer them architects who perform this task on a project basis. The actual workshop becomes more effective when you moderate and work off a list of concrete questions. Cutting the scheduled time in half brings additional focus.

On the upside, running architecture documentation workshops and *Sketching Bank Robbers* (20) can give you an invaluable set of system documentation that you can later use as a reference. I was planning to systematically conduct such sessions and create an architecture handbook that collects important architecture deci-sions across all systems in the IT landscape. This effort requires *good writing skills* (16) and adequate staffing, which you can only obtain by taking the *Architect Elevator* (2) to the upper floors and clearly articulating the value of documenting system architectures. For example, such documents could allow faster staff ramp-up, reveal architectural inconsistencies, and allow rational, fact-based decision making, which in turn supports evolution towards a harmonized IT landscape. In top-down organizations sometimes you have to lob things to the top so they can trickle back down.

No Free Pass

Occasionally, teams that are sent into architecture review would like to just obtain a "rubber stamp" for what they have done and aren't excited about you asking any questions at all. These are often the same candidates who answer the "why" questions with "because we have no time" after they purposefully waited until the very last minute. For such cases, I have a stated principle of "You can avoid my review, but you cannot get a free pass". If management decides that no architecture review is needed because they don't see architecture as a first-class citizen, I rather avoid the review altogether than hold a show trial.

I see this as in line with my professional reputation: we are tough but fair and make tasty hamburgers out of holy cows. My boss once summarized this in a nice compliment: she stated that she likes to have the architecture team involved because "we have nothing to sell, no one can fool us, and we take the time to explain things well." This would make a nice mandate for any architecture team.

If you wonder about the meaning of the German subtitle: it's from the title song of the German version of Sesame Street, which rhymes nicely and goes "Wieso, weshalb, warum, wer nicht fragt, bleibt dumm!", which literally translates into "why? who doesn't ask, remains stupid!" Don't remain stupid!

Architecture

Defining Architecture

There appear to be almost as many definitions of IT architecture as there are practicing architects. Most software architecture definitions cite a system's elements and components plus their interrelationships. In my view, this covers only one aspect of architecture. First, IT architecture is much more than software architecture: unless you outsourced all your IT infrastructure into the public cloud, you need to architect networks, data centers, computing infrastructure, storage, and much more. Second, defining which "components" you are focusing on constitutes a significant aspect of architecture.

 A manager once stated that he can't understand the many network issues despite all the network stuff "being there". His view was a physical one: Ethernet cables plugged into servers and switches. The complexity of network architecture, however, lies in virtual network segregation, routing, address translation, and much more.

Architecture as a Function

In large enterprises, the word "architecture" tends to describe both the structure of technical systems and an organizational unit: "we are setting up enterprise architecture." Most of my discussions on "architecture" focus on the system properties. For organizational aspects, I speak about "architects" - it's based on humans, after all.

There Always is an Architecture

It's worth pointing out that any system has an architecture, which puts statements like "we don't have time for architecture" into a questionable light. It's simply a matter of whether you consciously choose your architecture or whether you let it happen to you, with the latter invariably leading to the infamous *Big Ball of Mud*[20] architecture, also referred to as *Shanty Town*. While that architecture does allow for rapid implementation without central planning or specialized skills, it also tends to ignore critical infrastructure aspects and doesn't make for a great living environment. Fatalism isn't a great enterprise architecture strategy, so I suggest you pick your architecture.

The Value of Architecture

Because there always is an architecture, an organization should be clear on what it expects from setting up an architecture function. Setting up an architecture team and then not letting them do their job, for example by routinely subjecting architecture decisions to management decisions, is actually worse than intentionally letting things drift into a "big ball of mud": you pretend to define your architecture, but in reality you don't. Worse yet, good architects don't want to be in a place where architecture is seen as a form of corporate entertainment. If you don't take architecture seriously, you won't be able to attract and retain serious architects.

IT management often believes that "architecture" is a long-term investment that will only pay off far into the future. While this is true for some aspects, e.g. managed system evolution over time,

---

[20]http://www.laputan.org/mud/

architecture can also pay off in the short-term, e.g. when you can accommodate a customer requirement late in the development cycle, when you gain leverage in vendor negotiations because you avoided lock-in, or when you can easily migrate your systems to a new data center location. Good architecture can also make a team more productive by allowing concurrent development and testing of components. Generally, good architecture buys you flexibility. In a rapidly changing world, this seems like a smart investment.

As most upper management is well versed in financial models, I often describe investing in architecture as the equivalent to *buying an option*: an option gives the buyer the right, but not the obligation to execute on a contract, e.g. buying or selling a financial instrument, in the future. In IT architecture, the option allows you to make changes to the system design, the run-time platform, or functional capabilities. Just as in the financial world, options aren't free - the ability to act on a contract in the future, when more information is available, has a value and therefore a price. I don't think the *Black-Scholes model*[21] accurately computes the value of large-scale IT architecture, but it makes apparent that architecture has a measurable value and can therefore demand a price.

Principles Drive Decisions

Architecture is a matter of trade-offs: there rarely is one single "best" architecture. Architects therefore must take the context into consideration when making architectural decisions and aim to achieve conceptual integrity, i.e. uniformity across system designs. This is best accomplished by selecting a well-defined set of architecture principles which are consistently applied to architectural decisions. Deriving these principles from a declared architecture strategy assures that the decisions support the strategy.

---

[21]https://en.wikipedia.org/wiki/Black%E2%80%93Scholes_model

Vertical Cohesion

A good architecture is not only consistent across systems, but also considers all layers of a software and hardware stack. Investigating new types of scale-out compute hardware or software-defined networks is useful, but if all your applications are inflexible monoliths with hard-coded IP addresses you gain little. Architects therefore not only need to *Ride the Elevator* (2) across the organization but also up and down the technology stack.

Architecting the Real World

The real world is full of architectures; not just building architectures, but also cities, corporate organizations, or political systems. The real world has to deal with many of the same issues faced by large enterprises lack of central governance, difficult to reverse decisions, complexity, constant evolution, slow feedback cycles. Architects should walk through the world with open eyes, always looking to learn from the architectures they encounter.

When defining architecture in large organizations, architects need to know more than how to draw UML diagrams. They need to:

- gain architecture insights while *Waiting in the line at a Coffee Shop* (8).
- tell whether *Something Is Architecture* (9) in the first place.
- tackle complexity by *Thinking in Systems* (10).
- know that *Configuration isn't better than coding* (11).
- hunt zombies so they *Don't have their brain eaten* (12).
- navigate the IT landscape with an *Undistorted world map* (13).
- automate everything so that they *Never have to send a human to do a machine's job* (14).
- think like software developers as *Everything becomes software-defined* (15).

8. Your Coffee Shop Does Not Use 2-Phase Commit

Learn about distributed system design while in the queue!

Grande, durable, non-atomic, soy chai latte

Hotto Cocoa o Kudasai

You know you're a geek when going to the coffee shop gets you thinking about interaction patterns between loosely coupled systems. This happened to me on a trip to Japan. One of the more familiar sights in Tokyo is the insane number of Starbucks coffee shops, especially in the areas of Shinjuku and Roppongi.

While waiting for my "Hotto Cocoa" drink, I got thinking about how Starbucks processes drink orders. Starbucks, like most other businesses, is primarily interested in maximizing throughput of orders because more orders equal more revenue.

Interestingly, the optimization for throughput results in a concurrent and asynchronous processing model: when you place your order, the cashier marks a coffee cup with the details of your order (e.g. tall, non-fat, soy, dry, extra hot latte with double shot) and places it into the queue, which is quite literally a queue of coffee cups lined up on top of the espresso machine. This queue decouples cashier and barista, allowing the cashier to keep taking orders even if the barista is momentarily backed up. If the store gets busy, multiple baristas can be deployed in a *Competing Consumer*[22] scenario, meaning they work off items in parallel without duplicating work.

Asynchronous processing models can be highly scalable but are not without challenges. I started thinking about how Starbucks dealt with some of these challenges. Maybe we can learn something from the coffee shop about designing successful asynchronous messaging solutions?

Correlation

Parallel and asynchronous processing causes drink orders to be not necessarily completed in the same order in which they were placed. This can happen for two reasons. First, order processing time varies by type of beverage: a blended smoothie takes more time to prepare than a basic drip coffee. A drip coffee ordered last may thus arrive first. Second, baristas may make multiple drinks in one batch to optimize processing time.

Starbucks therefore has a correlation problem: drinks that are delivered out of sequence must be matched up to the correct

---

[22]http://www.enterpriseintegrationpatterns.com/patterns/messaging/
CompetingConsumers.html

customer. Starbucks solves the problem with the same "pattern" used in messaging architectures: a *Correlation Identifier*[23] uniquely marks each message and is carried through the processing steps. In the US, most Starbucks use an explicit correlation identifier by writing your name on the cup at the time of ordering, calling it out when the drink is ready. Other countries may correlate by the type of drink. When I had difficulties understanding the baristas calling out the types of drinks in Japan, my solution was to order extra large "venti" drinks because they're uncommon and therefore easily identifiable, that is, "correlatable."

Exception Handling

Exception handling in asynchronous messaging scenarios presents another challenge. What does the coffee shop do if you can't pay? They will toss the drink if it has already been made or otherwise pull your cup from the "queue". If they deliver you a drink that's incorrect or unsatisfactory, they will remake it. If the machine breaks down and they cannot make your drink, they will refund your money. Apparently, we can learn quite a bit about error handling strategies by standing in the queue!

Just like Starbucks, distributed systems often cannot rely on 2-phase-commit semantics that guarantee consistent outcomes across multiple actions. They therefore employ the same error handling strategies:

Write-off

This error handling strategy is the simplest of all: do nothing. If the error occurs during a single operation, you just ignore it. If the error happens during a sequence of related actions, you can ignore the error and continue with the subsequent steps, ignoring

---

[23]http://www.enterpriseintegrationpatterns.com/patterns/messaging/CorrelationIdentifier.html

or discarding any work done so far. This is what the coffee shop would do when a customer is unable to pay.

Doing nothing about an error might seem like a bad plan at first, but in the reality of a business transaction this option might be perfectly acceptable: if the loss is small, building an error correction solution is likely more expensive than just letting things be. When humans are involved, correcting errors also has a cost and may delay serving other customers. Moreover, error handling can lead to additional complexity – the last thing you want is an error handling mechanism that has errors. So, in many cases "simple does it."

For example, I worked for a number of ISP providers who would choose to *write-off* errors in the billing / provisioning cycle. As a result, a customer might end up with active service but would not get billed. The revenue loss was small enough that it didn't hurt the business and customers rarely complained about getting free service. Periodically, they would run reconciliation reports to detect the "free" accounts and close them.

Retry

When simply ignoring an error won't do, you may want to retry the failing operation. This is a plausible option if there's a realistic chance that a renewed attempt will actually succeed, for example because a temporary communications glitch has been fixed or an unavailable system has restarted. Retrying can overcome inter-mittent errors, but it doesn't help if the operation violates a firm business rule.

When encountering a failure in a group of operations (i.e. "trans-action"), things become simpler if all components are *idempotent*, meaning they can receive the same command multiple times without duplicating the execution. You can simply reissue all operations because the receivers that already completed them will simply ignore the retried operation. Shifting some of the error handling burden to the receivers thus simplifies the interaction.

Compensating Action

The final option to put the system back into a consistent state after a failed operation is to undo the operations that were completed so far. Such "compensating actions" work well for monetary transactions that can re-credit money that has been debited. If the coffee shop can't make the coffee to your satisfaction, they will refund your money to restore your wallet to its original state. Because real life is full of failures, compensating actions can take many forms, such as a business calling a customer to ask him to ignore a letter that has been sent or to return a package that was sent in error. The classic counter-example to compensating an action is sausage making. Some actions are not easily reversible.

Transactions

All of the strategies described so far differ from a two-phase commit that relies on separate *prepare* and *execute* phases. In the Starbucks example, a two-phase commit would equate to waiting at the cashier desk with the receipt and the money on the table until the drink is finished. Once the drink is added to the items on the table, money, receipt and drink can change hands in one swoop. Neither the cashier nor the customer would be able to leave until this "transaction" is completed.

Using such a two-phase-commit approach would eliminate the need for additional error handling strategies, but it would almost certainly hurt Starbucks' business because the number of customers they can serve within a certain time interval would decrease dramatically. This is a good reminder that a two-phase-commit can make life a lot simpler but it can also hurt the free flow of messages (and therefore the scalability) because it has to maintain stateful transaction resources across multiple, asynchronous actions. It's also an indication that a high-throughput system should be optimized for the happy path instead of burdening each transaction for the rare case when something goes wrong.

Backpressure

Despite working asynchronously, the coffee shop cannot scale infinitely. As the queue of labeled coffee cups gets longer and longer, Starbucks can temporarily reassign a cashier to work as barista. This helps reduce the wait time for customers who have already placed an order while exerting *backpressure* to customers still waiting to place their order. No one likes waiting in line, but not yet having placed your order provides you with the option to leave the store and forgo the coffee or to wander to the next, not-very-far-away coffee shop.

Conversations

The coffee shop interaction is also a good example of a simple, but common *Conversation Pattern*[24], which illustrates sequences of message exchanges between participants. The interaction between two parties (customer and coffee shop) consists of a short synchronous interaction (ordering and paying) and a longer, asynchronous interaction (making and receiving the drink). This type of conversation is quite common in purchasing scenarios. For example, when placing an order on Amazon the short synchronous interaction assigns an order number while all subsequent steps (charging credit card, packaging, shipping) are performed asynchronously. You are notified via e-mail (asynchronous) when the additional steps complete. If anything goes wrong, Amazon usually compensates (refunding your credit card) or retries (resending lost goods).

Canonical Data Model

A coffee shop can teach you even more about distributed system design. When Starbucks was relatively new, customers were both

---

[24]http://www.enterpriseintegrationpatterns.com/patterns/conversation/

enamored and frustrated by the new language they had to learn just to order a coffee. Small coffees are now "tall", while a large one is called "venti". Defining your own language is not only a clever marketing strategy, but also establishes a *Canonical Data Model*[25] that optimizes downstream processing. Any uncertainties (soy or non-fat?) are resolved right at the "user interface" by the cashier and thus avoid a lengthy dialog that would burden the barista.

Welcome to the Real World!

The real world is mostly asynchronous: our daily lives consist of many coordinated, but asynchronous interactions, such as reading and replying to e-mail, buying coffee etc. This means that an asynchronous messaging architecture can often be a natural way to model these types of interactions. It also means that looking at daily life can help design successful messaging solutions. Domo arigato gozaimasu!

---

[25]http://www.enterpriseintegrationpatterns.com/patterns/messaging/
CanonicalDataModel.html

9. Is this Architecture?

Look for decisions!

Would you pay an architect for this?

Part of my job as Chief Architect is to review and approve system architectures. When I ask teams to show me "their architecture", I frequently don't consider what I receive an architecture document. The counter-question "what do you expect?" isn't so easy for me to answer: despite many formal definitions, it isn't immediately clear what architecture is or whether a document really depicts an architecture. Too often we have to fall back to the "I know it when I see it" test famously applied to obscene material by the Supreme Court. We'd hope that identifying architecture is a more noble task than identifying obscene material, so let's try a little harder. I am not a big believer in all-encompassing definitions but prefer to use lists of defining characteristics or tests that can be applied. One of my favorite tests for architecture documentation is whether it contains any non-trivial decisions and the rationale behind them.

Defining Software Architecture

Enough attempts at defining software architecture have been made that the Software Engineering Institute (SEI) maintains a reference page of software architecture definitions[26].

The most widely used definitions include the one from Garlan and Perry from 1995:

> *The structure of the components of a system, their inter-relationships, and principles and guidelines governing their design and evolution over time*

In 2000 the ANSI/IEEE Std 1471 chose the following definition: (adopted as ISO/IEC 42010 in 2007):

> *The fundamental organization of a system, embodied in its components, their relationships to each other and the environment, and the principles governing its design and evolution*

The Open Group adopted a variation thereof for TOGAF:

> *The structure of the components, their interrelation-ships, and principles and guidelines governing their design and evolution over time*

One of my personal favorites is from Desmond D'Souza's and Alan Cameron Wills' book[27]:

> *Design decisions about any system that keep implemen-tors and maintainers from exercising needless creativity*

---

[26]http://www.sei.cmu.edu/architecture/start/glossary/bibliographicdefs.cfm

[27]D'Souza, Wills: Objects, Components, and Frameworks with UML: The Catalysis(SM) Approach; Addison-Wesley Professional, 1998

The key point here isn't that architecture should dampen all creativity, but *needless* creativity, of which I witness ample amounts. It also highlights the importance of _making decisions _ (6).

Architectural Decisions

These well-thought-out definitions aren't easy to apply, though, when someone walks up with a PowerPoint slide showing boxes *and lines* (22), claiming "this is my system architecture". The first test I tend to apply is whether the documentation contains meaningful decisions. After all, if no decisions needed to be made, why employ an architect and prepare architectural documentation?

Martin Fowler's knack for explaining the essence of things using extremely simple examples motivated me to illustrate the "architectural decision test" with the simplest example I could think of, drawing from the (admittedly limping) analogy to building architecture. I even took it upon myself to supply the artwork to make sure things end up about as basic as one could wish for and to pay homage to Christopher Alexander's Pattern Sketches[28].

Is this architecture?

---

[28]Alexander: A Pattern Language: Towns, Buildings, Construction; Oxford University Press, 1977

Consider the drawing of a house on the left. It has many of the elements required by the popular definitions of systems architecture: we see the main *components of the system* (door, windows, roof) and their *interrelationships* (door and windows in the wall, roof on the top). We might be a tad thin, though, on *principles governing its design*, but we do notice that we have a single door that reaches the ground and multiple windows, which follows common building principles.

Yet, to build such a house I wouldn't want to pay an architect. This house is "cookie-cutter", meaning I don't see any non-obvious decisions that an architect would have made. Consequently, I wouldn't consider this architecture.

Let's compare this to the sketch on the right-hand side. The sketch is equally simple and poorly drawn and the house is almost the same, except for the roof. This house has a steep roof and for a good reason: the house is designed for a cold climate where winters bring extensive snowfall. Snow is quite heavy and can easily overload the roof of the house. A steep roof allows the snow to slide off or be easily removed thanks to gravity, a pretty cheap and widely available resource. Additionally, an overhang prevents the sliding snow from piling up right in front of the windows.

To me, this is architecture: non-trivial decisions have been made and documented. The decisions are driven by the system context, in this case, the climate: it's unlikely that the customer explicitly stated a requirement that the roof not be crushed. Additionally, the documentation highlights relevant decisions and omits unnecessary noise.

If you believe these architectural decisions were pretty obvious, let's look at a very different house:

Great architecture on a napkin

This house was designed for a different climate, a hot and sunny one, which allows the walls to be made out of glass as insulation against low temperatures is less of a concern. However, walls of glass have the problem that the sun heats up the building, making it feel more like a greenhouse than a residence. The solution? Extending the roof well beyond the glass walls keeps the interior in the shade, especially in summer when the sun is high in the sky. In the winter, when the sun is low on the horizon, the sun reaches through the windows and helps warm the building interior. Also, a flat roof with an overhang isn't a problem in this climate. Again, the architecture is defined by a fairly simple, but fundamental decision documented in an easy-to-understand format that highlights the essence of the decision and the rationale behind it.

Fundamental Decisions Don't Need to be Complicated

If you think the idea of building an overhanging roof isn't all that original or significant, try buying one of the first homes to feature such a design, e.g. the Case Study House No 22 in Los Angeles by architect Pierre Koenig. It's easily in the league of most recognized residential building in Los Angeles or beyond (aided by Julius Shulman's iconic photograph) and surely isn't for sale. You can tour it, though, if you sign up far in advance. Significant architecture decisions may look obvious in hindsight but that doesn't diminish their value. No one is perfect, though: UCLA PhD students have measured that the overhang works better on the south-facing facade than west or east[29].

Fit for Purpose

The simple house example also highlights another important property of architecture: rarely is an architecture simply "good" or "bad". Rather, architecture is fit or unfit for purpose. A house with glass walls and a flat roof may be regarded as great architecture, but probably not in the Swiss Alps where it will collapse after a few winters or suffer from a leaking roof. It also doesn't do much good near the equator where the sun's path on the sky remains fairly constant throughout the year. In those regions, you are better off with thick walls, small windows, and lots of air conditioning.

Assessing the context and identifying implicit constraints or assumptions in proposed designs is an architect's key responsibility. Sometimes, architects are described as the people dealing with non-functional requirements. I find that more often than not architects have to deal with *non-requirements*, implicit needs or assumptions that weren't communicated at all.

Even the dreaded Big Ball of Mud[30] can be "fit for purpose", e.g. when you need to make a deadline at all cost and can't care much about what happens afterwards. This may not be the context you wish for, but just like houses in some regions have to be earthquake proof, some architectures have to be management-proof.

Passing the Test

Having stretched the overused building architecture analogy one more time, how do we translate it back to software systems architecture? Systems architecture doesn't have to be something terribly

---

29La Roche: The Case Study House Program in Los Angeles: A Case for Sustainability; in Proc. of Conference on Passive and Low Energy Architecture, 2002
[30]http://www.laputan.org/mud/

complicated. It must include, however, significant decisions that are well documented and are based on a clear rationale. The word "significant" may be open to some interpretation and depend on the level of sophistication of the organization, but "we separate front-end from back-end code" or "we use monitoring" surely have the ring of "my door reaches the ground so people can walk in" or "I put windows in the walls so light can enter". Instead, when discussing architectures let's talk about what isn't obvious or something that involved heavy trade-offs. For example, "do you use a service layer and why?" (some people may find even this obvious) or "why do you use a session-oriented conversation protocol?"

It's quite amazing how many "architecture documents" don't pass this relatively simple test. I hope using the building analogy provides a simple and non-threatening way to provide feedback and to motivate architects to better document their designs and decisions.

10. Every System is Perfect...

...for what it was designed to do!

Analyzing system behavior

Much of what architects do is reason about the behavior of *complex systems*, systems that have many pieces and complex interrelationships. There's a whole field dedicated to such reasoning, called *Systems Thinking* or *Complex Systems Theory*. While popular software architecture definitions (see *Is This Architecture?* (9)) focus on a system's components and interrelationships, systems thinking emphasizes behavior, viewing structure simply as a means to achieve a desired behavior.

Heater as a System

A residential heater provides a canonical example of a *system* (which we also look at when we realize that *Control is an illusion* (23)). A heating system's typical architecture diagram would depict the components and their relationships: a furnace generates hot water or air, a radiator or air duct delivers the heat to the room, and a thermostat controls the furnace. The control system theory point-of-view considers the thermostat the central element: it switches the furnace on and off as needed to regulate the room temperature.

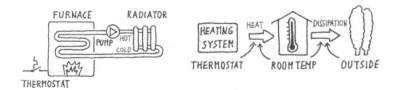

A structural view (left) and a systems view (right) of a heater

In contrast, the systems thinking point of view focuses on the room temperature as the central variable and reasons about how it is influenced: the burning furnace increases the room temperature while heat dissipation to the outside reduces it. Heat dissipation depends on both the room and the outside temperature: in cold weather more heat dissipates through walls and windows. That's why smart heating systems increase the heating power in cold weather. In a way, systems thinking is a parallel universe that looks at the same system from a completely different angle.

Feedback Loops

Systems thinking helps us understand interrelated behavior, for example feedback loops. The room thermostat establishes a negative feedback loop, which is typical for control systems: if the room temperature is too high, the furnace turns off, letting the room cool down again. Negative feedback loops usually aim to keep a system in a relatively stable state – the room temperature will still oscillate slightly depending on the hysteresis of the thermostat and the inertia of the heating system. The self-stabilizing range of most systems is limited, though: a heater cannot cool a room in the heat of summer or compensate for an open window during winter.

Positive feedback loops behave in the opposite way: an increase in one system variable fuels a further increase. We know the dramatic effects of such behavior from explosives (heat releases more oxygen to burn hotter), nuclear reactions (a classical "chain reaction"), or hyperinflation (a spiral of price and wage increases). Another positive feedback loop consists of more cars on the road leading to investments in roads as opposed to public transit, which makes it more compelling to commute by car. Likewise, rich people tend to have more investment options to achieve higher returns, leading to a "the rich getting richer" symptom, as for example described in Piketty's *Capital in the Twenty-First Century*[31].

Positive feedback loops can be dangerous due to their "explosive" nature. Policies are often designed to counteract such positive feedback loops with negative ones, e.g. by taxing rich people more heavily or by increasing gasoline tax while subsidizing public transit. However, it's difficult to balance out the exponential character of positive feedback loops. Thinking in systems helps us reason about such effects.

Organized Complexity

Gerald Weinberg[32] highlighted the importance of thinking in systems by dividing the world into three areas: *organized simplicity* is the realm of well-understood mechanics, such as levers or electrical systems consisting of discrete resistors and capacitors. You can calculate exactly how these systems behave. On the other end of the

[31]Piketty: Capital in the Twenty-First Century, Belknap Press, 2014
[32]Weinberg: An Introduction to General Systems Thinking, Dorset House, 2001

spectrum, *unorganized complexity* doesn't allow us to understand exactly what's going on, but we can model the system as a whole statistically because the behavior is unorganized, meaning the parts don't interrelate much. Modeling the spread of a virus falls into this category. The tricky domain is the one of *organized complexity*, where structure and interaction between components matter, but the system is too complex to solve it by using a formula. This is the area of systems. And the area of systems architecture.

System Effects

If we can't determine system behavior with mathematical formulas, how can systems thinking help us? Complex systems, especially systems involving humans, tend to be subject to recurring system effects or patterns. These effects explain why fishermen keep over-fishing, depleting their own livelihood, and why tourists flocking to the same destination destroy exactly what attracted them. Understanding these patterns allows us to better predict system behavior and influence it. Donella Meadows' book *Thinking in Systems*[33] contains a list of common effects, including these typical ones:

- *Bounded Rationality*, a term coined by Nobel laureate Herbert A. Simon, captures the effect that people will generally do what is rational, but only within the context which they observe. For example, if an apartment building has a central heating system without consumption-based billing, people will leave the heater on all day and open the windows to cool down the apartment as needed. Obviously, this is a giant waste of energy and leads to pollution, resource depletion, and global warming. However, if your bounded context is just that of the temperature in your apartment and your wallet, this behavior is the rational thing to do, whether you like it or not: keeping the heater running allows you to control the

---

[33]Meadows: Thinking in Systems, Chelsea Green Publishing, 2008

room temperature more easily as you avoid the inertia of the heating system having to warm up.

- The *Tragedy of the Commons* derives from *the commons*, a shared pasture in old villages that was open to all farmers' animals. As this resource is free, the farmers are incentivized to acquire more cattle to feed on the commons. Of course, as the commons is a finite resource, this behavior will lead to resource depletion and poverty, hence the tragedy. One reason such a system doesn't self-regulate is delay: the effect of the wrong behavior will only become apparent when it is too late.

John Gall's *Systems Bible*[34] gives a humorous, but also insightful account of the ways in which systems behave, often against our intention or intuition.

Understanding System Behavior

Systems documentation, especially in IT, tends to depict the static structure, but rarely the behavior of the system. Ironically, the system's behavior is what's most interesting, though: systems generally exist to exhibit a certain, desirable behavior. For example, the heating system was created to keep the temperature in your house at a comfortable level. Server infrastructure is made redundant to increase availability. In both cases the system structure is simply a means to an end.

The difficulty in deriving system behavior from its components can be illustrated by the heating system in my apartment, which supplies both floor heating and wall radiators with hot water and comprises a handful of major components: the gas burner heats the water inside a primary circuit driven by a built-in pump. Two additional external pumps feed the hot water from the primary circuit to the floor heating and wall radiators, respectively. A

---

[34]Gall: The Systems Bible, Third Edition, General Systemantics Press, 2002

misconfiguration caused the secondary pumps to not draw enough water, and therefore heat, from the primary circuit, which quickly overheated. This, in turn, caused the gas heater to shut off for a fixed duration, leading to a lack of heating power: naturally, the house cannot get warm when the heater is not burning. Because the house wouldn't warm up, the technician's intuition was to *increase* the burner's heating power. However, this only exacerbated the problem: the system wasn't able to move enough heat away from the primary circuit, so increasing the gas burner's power only overheated it faster. After almost a dozen attempts, the heating system still isn't operating as designed because the technicians may understand the individual system components, but not the complex system behavior.

Seems a little complicated? For architects, this stuff is our daily bread and butter. Understanding complex interrelationships between system components and influencing them to achieve a desired behavior is what architects do. Often a *Good Diagram* (21) will help.

Influencing System Behavior

Most of what users see from a system are events: things happening as a result of the system behavior, which in turn is determined by the system structure, that is often invisible. If the users are unhappy with those events, such as the heater shutting off despite the room being cold, they often try to inflict a change, such as setting the room thermostat higher, without analyzing or changing the system behind them. The book *Inviting Disaster*[35] provides dramatic examples of how misunderstanding a system led to major catastrophes such as the Three-mile-island nuclear reactor incident or the capsizing of the Deepwater Horizon drilling platform. In both cases, compromised system displays led operators to perform the very action that caused the disaster because they didn't understand

---

[35]Chiles: Inviting Disaster, Harper Business, 2002

the underlying system and its behavior from the events they observed. Their *mental model* deviated from the real system, causing them to make fatal decisions.

It has repeatedly been observed that humans are particularly bad at steering systems that have slow feedback loops, i.e. that exhibit reactions to changing inputs only after a significant delay. Overuse of credit cards is a classic example. Also, humans are prone to taking actions that have the opposite of the intended effect. For example, people react to overly full work calendars by setting up "blockers", which make the calendars even fuller. Instead, one needs to understand and fix what causes the full calendars, for example, a misaligned organizational structure that requires too many alignment meetings. You can't fix a system by merely addressing the symptoms.

Understanding system effects can help you devise more effective ways to influence the system and thus its behavior. For example, transparency is a useful antidote to the bounded rationality effect because it widens peoples' bounds. An example from Donella Meadows' book illustrates that having the electricity meter visible in the hallway caused people to be more conservative with their energy consumption without additional rules or penalties. Interestingly, systems thinking can be applied to both organizational and technical systems. We'll learn this, for example, when we *Scale an Organization* (26).

Systems Resist Change

Changing systems is difficult, not only because their complex structure, but also because most of them actively resist change. Organizational systems' change resistance achieves longevity, e.g. through well-defined processes, but presents a challenge when a shift in the environment requires the organization to change. Frederic Laloux[36] describes it as a key characteristic of *amber*

---

[36]Laloux: Reinventing Organizations, Nelson Parker, 2014

organizations: they are built on the assumption that what worked in the past will work in the future, and it often served them well over thousands of years.

 As described in *Question Everything* (7) if you request better documentation for architecture reviews, "the system" may respond by scheduling lengthy workshops that drain your available time. If you increase pressure, the system will respond with sub-quality documentation that increases your review cycles. You must therefore get to the root of the problem and highlight the value of good documentation, properly train architects, and allocate time for this task in project schedules.

Most organizational systems have settled into a steady state over time and serve their purpose well enough. If the business environment demands a different system behavior, the system will actively resist by wanting to revert to its previous state. It's like trying to push a car out of a ditch: the car keeps rolling back until you finally get it over the hump. This system effect makes organizational transformation so challenging.

11. Code Fear Not!

Programming in a poorly designed language without tool support is no fun

Who dares run this code?

Yoda, the wise teacher of Jedi apprentice Luke Skywalker in the Star Wars movies, knows that fear leads to anger; anger leads to hate; hate leads to suffering. Likewise, Corporate IT's fear of code and the love of configuration can lead it down a path to suffering that is difficult to escape from. Beware of the dark side, which has many faces, including vendors peddling products that "only require configuration", as opposed to tedious, error-prone coding. Sadly, most complex configuration really is just programming, albeit in a poorly designed, rather constrained language without decent tooling or useful documentation.

Fear of Code

Corporate IT, which is often driven by operational considerations, tends to consider code the stuff that contains all the bugs, causes performance problems, and is written by *expensive external consultants* (34) who are difficult to hold liable as they'll have long moved to another project by the time the problems surface. Corporate IT's fear of code plays to the advantage of enterprise vendors who tout configuration over coding with slogans like "this tool does not require programming, everything is done through configuration." The most grotesque example of fear of code I have observed had corporate IT providing application servers that carry no operational support once you deploy code on it. It's like voiding a car's warranty after you start the engine - after all, the manufacturer has no idea what you will do to it!

Good Intentions

Buying off-the-shelf solutions and customizing / configuring them can save IT departments a lot of time and money: letting third-party tools do the grunt work not only saves effort, it also lets you benefit from regular updates and security patches. Libraries and tools are also often accompanied by a community that lowers the barrier to entry for a new technology. For example, why would you want to write your own XML serializer to expose a service API?

Levels of Abstraction

The primary technique that makes developers' lives easier is to raise the level of abstraction at which they work. Very few programmers still write assembly code, read single data blocks from a disk, or put individual packets onto the network. This level of detail has been nicely wrapped behind high-level languages, files and socket streams. These programming abstractions are very convenient and dramatically increase productivity: try doing without them! If abstractions are this useful, one may legitimately wonder whether adding another abstraction layer can boost productivity even further. Ultimately, if a system provides sufficient abstraction, can it do away with coding altogether and allow solution development simply by configuration?

Simplicity vs. Flexibility

When trying to raise the level of programming abstraction, one faces a fundamental dilemma: how to make a really simple model without losing too much flexibility? If the developer wants to store individual data records on the hard disk, for example to create a rapid direct-access indexing system, the file stream abstraction is actually in the way. The best abstractions are those that solve and encapsulate the difficult part of the problem, but still leave the user with sufficient flexibility. If the abstraction takes away too many or the wrong things, it's not useful. If it takes away too few things, it did not accomplish much in terms of simplifying the programming effort. Or as Alan Kay elegantly stated[37]: Simple things should be simple, complex things should be possible.

MapReduce is a positive example: it encapsulates and thus abstracts away the difficult parts of distributed data processing, such as controlling and scheduling many worker instances, dealing with failed nodes, aggregating data, etc. But it nevertheless leaves the programmer enough flexibility to solve a wide range of problems.

Packaging the Abstraction

Vendors showing shiny drag-and-drop demos can make us believe that painting a thin visual veneer over an existing programming model can provide a higher level of abstraction. However, when talking about programming abstraction we must distinguish

---

[37]https://en.m.wikiquote.org/wiki/Alan_Kay

the *model* from the *representation*. A complex model, such as workflow, which includes concepts like concurrency, long-running transactions, compensation, etc., carries heavy conceptual weight, even when wrapped in a pretty visual packaging. This is not to say visual representations have no value. Especially in the case of workflow, visual representations are quite expressive. But they cannot wave a magic wand that makes the challenges of workflow design go away.

Visual programming may initially appear to increase productivity but generally does not scale very well. Once applications grow, it becomes difficult to follow what's going on. Debugging and version control can also be a nightmare. I generally apply two tests when vendors provide a demo of visual programming tools:

1. I ask them to enter a typo into one of the fields where the user is expected to enter some logic. Often this leads to cryptic error messages or obscure errors in generated code down the line. I call this "tightrope programming": as long as you stay exactly on the line, everything is well. One misstep and the deep abyss awaits you.
2. I ask them to leave the room for 2 minutes while we change a few random elements of their demo configuration. Upon return, they would have to debug and figure out what was changed. No vendor was ever willing to take the challenge.

Configuration

What level of abstraction deserves to be called "configuration" versus "high-level programming"? Aforementioned vendor demos may lead us to believe that everything that has a visual user interface or uses XML (or JSON or YAML) is configuration. However, anyone who has programmed in XSLT, which is contained in XML files, can attest that this isn't configuration, but heavy-duty declarative programming.

Code or Data?

A better decision criterion could be whether what you provide to the system is executable or just a piece of data. If the algorithm is predefined and you only supply a few key values, it may be fair to call this configuration. For example, let's assume a program needs to classify users into children, adults, and seniors. The code will contain a chain of `if-else` or a `switch` statement. A configuration file could now supply the values for the decision thresholds, e.g. 18 and 65. This would fit our definition of configuration. It would also imply that changing the values is safe: typing in a number saves you from having to understand operator precedence or from introducing syntax errors. Alas, it does not save you from screwing up the program. If you accidentally enter the values 65 and 18, the program is likely to be not working as expected. The exact program behavior in this case is impossible to predict as it depends on the way the algorithm is coded. If the program checks for children first, you may have declared everyone as a child whereas if the program checks for seniors first, you may have made everyone a senior. So while configuration is safer, it's not foolproof.

DSL designers would rightly state that the correct way to configure such program behavior is a decision table, which can in fact be rendered in modern DSL-aware code editors. Here, the distinction between coding and configuration blurs, but one has to admit that a decision table is likely more expressive and less error prone than entering two decimals, which by themselves do not express any semantics.

The distinction between code and data blurs further when the data you enter determines execution order. For example, the "data" you enter may be a sequence of instruction codes. Or the data may resemble a declarative programming language, for example to configure a rules engine or even XSLT. Aren't coding instructions just data for the execution engine? Apparently, it's not so black-and-white.

Run-time vs. Design-time

The next assumption about configuration is that it generally can
be changed after the code is finished, tested, and deployed. As
we just saw above, this does not imply that configuration doesn't
have to be tested. The underlying assumption here is that changing
code is slow (because you have to rebuild and redeploy the whole
application) and risky (as you may be introducing new defects).
Interpreted languages, microservices architectures, and automated
build- and deployment chains put quite a few question marks behind these assumptions. This doesn't mean configuration is useless,
but it means that we now have tools that allow us to achieve much
of what configuration was intended to do without having to decide
a priori what decisions must be made during program construction
vs. those that can be made at a later time. So the next time a
vendor touts configuration you can challenge them to speed up their
software delivery model.

Tooling

As we have seen, the boundary between configuring and programming at a high level of abstraction is very fuzzy. When you consider
yourself to be programming, you usually assume to be having
proper tool support like editors, syntax validation, refactoring,
version control, diff, etc. Frequently these tools are not available
when doing configuration.

For example, when designing messaging architectures, individual
components are composed into a solution by connecting them via
named message channels. "Configuration" files would determine
which channel(s) a component receives messages from and which
channel(s) it sends messages to. Storing this data in local XML
configuration files seemed convenient, but is prone to misconfiguration: components would not talk to each other because of
mismatching channel names or because the right components were

chained together in the wrong order. Composing a messaging system is not a matter of simple configuration files, but a high-level programming model for the *composition layer* of the system. Treating the config files as first class citizens by checking them into source control and by creating validation and management tools, can help debugging and troubleshooting enormously. The lack of such tooling is a major problem for complex configurations.

Configuration Programming

Whenever there's a choice to be made, in our case *programming* vs. *configuration*, you can be assured that someone has found a compromise. In our case this would be Configuration Programming[38]: An approach that advocates the use of a separate configuration language to specify the coarse-grained structure of programs. Configuration programming is particularly attractive for concurrent, parallel and distributed systems that have inherently complex program structures.

Any Place for Configuration?

So is there a good place for configuration? I have seen appropriate uses of configuration, for example to inject run-time parameters to distributed service instances. Interestingly, in that specific case the configuration parameters were computed by a functional programming language, called Borg Configuration Language[39]. So I guess it's a blurry line after all.

Abstractions are a very useful thing, but believing that calling the abstraction "configuration" is going to eliminate complexity or the need to hire developers is a common fallacy. Instead, treat configuration as a first-class citizen that requires design, testing, version control, and deployment management just like code. Otherwise,

---

[38]http://foldoc.org/configuration%20programming
[39]https://ai.google/research/pubs/pub43438

you have created a proprietary, poorly designed, language without tooling support.

12. If You Never Kill Anything, You Will Live Among Zombies

And they will eat your brain.

The night of the living legacy systems

Corporate IT lives among zombies: old systems that are half alive and have everyone in fear of going anywhere near them. They are also tough to kill completely. Worse yet, they eat IT staff's brains. It's like *Shaun of the Dead* minus the funny parts.

Legacy

Legacy systems are built on outdated technology and are often poorly documented, but (ostensibly) still perform important business functions – in many cases, the exact scope of the function they perform is not completely known. Systems often fall into the state of legacy because technology moves faster than the business: life insurance systems often must maintain data and functionality for decades, rendering much of the technology used to build the system obsolete. With a bit of luck, the systems don't have to be updated anymore, so IT may be inclined to "simply let it run", following the popular advice to "never touch a running system". However, changing regulations or security vulnerabilities in old versions of the application or the underlying software stack are likely to interfere with such an approach.

Traditional IT sometimes justifies their zombies with having to support the business: how can you shut down a system that may be needed by the business? They also feel that digital companies don't have such problems because they are too young to have accumulated legacy. 150 Google developers attending Mike Feathers' talk about *Working Effectively with Legacy Code*[40] might make us question this assumption. Because Google's systems evolve rapidly, they also accumulate legacy more quickly than traditional IT. So it's not that they have been blessed with not having legacy, they must have found a way to deal with it.

Fear of Change

Systems become legacy zombies by not evolving with the technology. This happens in classic IT largely because change is seen as a risk. Once again: "never touch a running system". System releases are based on extensive test cycles that can last months, making updates or changes a costly endeavor. Worse yet, there's no "business

---

[40]Michael Feathers: Working Effectively with Legacy Code, Prentice Hall, 2004

case" for updating the system technology. This widespread logic is about as sound as considering changing the oil in your car a waste of money - after all the car still runs if you don't. And it even makes your quarterly profit statement look a little better, that is, until the engine seizes.

A team from Credit Suisse described how to counterbalance this trap in their aptly titled book *Managed Evolution*[41]. The key driver for managed evolution is to maintain agility in a system. A system that no one wants to touch has no agility at all - it can't be changed. In a very static business and technology environment, this may not be all that terrible. Today's environment is everything but stable, though, rendering the inability to change a system into a major liability for IT and the business.

Most things are the way they are for a reason. This is also true for the fear of change in corporate IT. These organizations typically lack the tools, processes, and skills to closely observe production metrics and to rapidly deploy fixes in case something goes awry. Hence they focus on trying to test for all scenarios before deploying and then running the application more or less "blind", hoping that nothing breaks. Jeff Sussna describes the necessity to break out of this conundrum very nicely in his great book *Designing Delivery*[42].

Version Upgrades

The zombie problem is not limited to systems written in PL/1 running on an IBM/360, though. Often updating basic runtime infrastructures like application servers, JDK versions, browsers, or operating systems scare the living daylights out of IT, causing version updates to be deferred until the vendor ceases support. The natural reaction then is to pay the vendor to extend support because anything is less painful than having to migrate your software to a new version.

---

[41]Murer, Bonati: Managed Evolution: A Strategy for Very Large Information Systems, Springer, 2011

[42]Jeff Sussna: Designing Delivery, O'Reilly, 2015

Often the inability to migrate cascades across multiple layers of the software stack: one cannot upgrade to a newer JDK because it doesn't run on the current application server version, which can't be updated because it requires a new version of the operating system which deprecates some library or feature the software depends on. I have seen IT shops that are stuck on Internet Explorer 6 because their software utilizes a proprietary feature not present in later versions. Looking at the user interfaces of most corporate applications, one finds it difficult to imagine that they eked out every little bit of browser capability. They surely would have been better off not depending on such a peculiar feature and instead being able to benefit from browser evolution. Such a line of thought does require a "change is good" mindset, though.

Ironically, IT's widespread *fear of code* (11) can lead them to buy into large frameworks, which in turn make version upgrades tough and increase the chance of growing zombies. Anyone who has done an SAP upgrade can relate.

Run vs. Change

The fear of change is even encoded in many IT organizations that separate "run" (operating) from "change" (development), making it clear that running software does not imply change. Rather, it's the opposite of change, which is done by application development - those guys who produce the flaky code IT is afraid of. Structuring IT teams this way will guarantee that systems will age and become legacy because no change could be applied to them.

One may think that by not changing running systems, IT can keep the operational cost low. Ironically, the opposite is true: many IT departments spend more than half of their IT budget on "run" and "maintenance", leaving only a fraction of the budget for "change" that can support the evolving demands of the business. That's because running and supporting legacy applications is expensive: operational processes are often manual; the software may not be stable, necessitating constant attention; the software may not scale well, requiring the procurement of expensive hardware; lack of documentation means time-consuming trial-and-error troubleshooting in case of problems. These are reasons why legacy systems tie up valuable IT resources and skills, effectively devouring the brains of IT that could be applied to more useful tasks, for example delivering features to the business.

Planned Obsolescence

When selecting a product or conducting a request for proposal (RfP), classic IT tends to compile a list containing dozens or hundreds of features or capabilities that a candidate product has to offer. Often, these lists are compiled by external consultants unaware of the business need or the company's IT strategy. However, they tend to create long lists and longer appears to be better to some IT staff. To cite another car analogy, this is a bit like evaluating a car by having an endless list of more or less (ir)relevant features like "must have a 12V lighter outlet", "speedometer goes above 200 km/h", "can turn the front wheels" and then scoring a BMW vs. a Mercedes for these. How likely this is to steer (pun intended) you towards the car you will enjoy the most is questionable.

Worse, one item routinely missing from such "features" lists is planned obsolescence: how easy is it to replace the system? Can the data be exported in a well-defined format? Can business logic be extracted and re-used in a replacement system to avoid vendor lock-in? During the new product selection honeymoon this may feel like discussing a prenup before the wedding - who likes to think about parting ways when you are about to embark on a lifelong journey? In the case of an IT system, you better hope the journey isn't lifelong - systems are meant to come and go. So better have a prenup in place than being held hostage by the system (or vendor) you are trying to part with.

If it hurts, do it more often

How to break out of the "change is bad" cycle? As mentioned before, without proper instrumentation and automation, making changes is not only scary but indeed risky. The reluctance to upgrade or migrate software is similar to the reluctance to build and test software often. Martin Fowler issued the best advice to break this cycle: "if it hurts, do it more often". No, this is not meant to appeal to masochistic IT staff, but it highlights that deferring a painful task generally makes it disproportionately more painful: if you haven't built your source code in months, it's guaranteed not to go smoothly. Likewise, if you are 3 versions of an application server behind, you'll have the migration from hell.

Performing such tasks more frequently provides a forcing function to automate some of the processes, e.g. with automated builds or test suites. Dealing with migration problems will also become routine. This is the reason emergency workers train regularly - otherwise, they'll freak out in case of an actual emergency and won't be effective. Of course, training takes time and energy. But what's the alternative?

Culture of Change

Digital companies also have to deal with change and obsolescence. The going joke at Google was that every API had two versions: the obsolete one and the not-yet-quite-ready one. Actually, it wasn't a joke, but pretty close to reality. Dealing with this was often painful - every piece of code you wrote could break at any time because of changes in the dependencies. But living this culture of change allows Google to *keep the pace up* (31) - the most important of today's IT capabilities. Sadly, it's rarely listed as a performance indicator. Even Shaun knows that zombies can't run fast.

13. The IT World is Flat

Without a map, any road looks promising

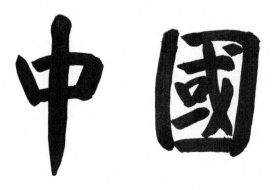

Living in the Middle Kingdom

Maps have been valuable tools for millennia, despite most of them, especially world maps, being quite badly distorted. The fundamental challenge of plotting the surface of a sphere onto a flat sheet of paper forces maps to make compromises when depicting angles, sizes, and distances - if the earth was flat, things would be much easier. For example, the historically popular *Mercator projection* provides true angles for seafarers, meaning you can read an angle off the map and use the same angle on the ship's compass (compensating for the discrepancy between geographic and magnetic north). The price to pay for this convenient property, which avoids distorting angles, is area distortion – the further away countries are from the equator, the larger they appear on the map. That's why Africa looks disproportionately small on such maps[43], a trade-off that may be acceptable when navigating by boat: misestimating the distance is likely a lesser problem than heading into the wrong direction.

Plotting the surface of a sphere also presents the challenge of deciding where the "middle" is. Most world maps conveniently position Europe in the center, supported by 0 degree longitude (the *prime meridian*) going through Greenwich, UK. This depiction results in Asia being in the "East" and the Americas being in the "West". The keen observer will quickly conclude that when living on a sphere, notions of West and East are somewhat relative to the viewpoint of the beholder. The same type of thinking likely motivated East Asia residents to historically put their country in the middle of the map and even name it accordingly: 中國 – middle kingdom.

While many centuries later we may regard such a world view as a tad self-centered, at the time it simply made practical sense: having the most detail about places that are near you makes putting your starting point in the middle of your map natural. It also lines up the map boundaries with your travel limits.

IT landscapes are also vast and navigating a typical enterprise's range of products and technologies can be equally daunting to sailing Cape Horn. Despite some similarities, each IT landscape tends to be its own planet, making universal IT world maps hard to come by. Aside from some useful attempts like the Big Data Landscape by Matt Turck[44], enterprise architects therefore often rely on maps provided by their vendors.

---

[43]http://www.informationisbeautiful.net/2010/the-true-size-of-africa
[44]http://mattturck.com/2014/05/11/the-state-of-big-data-in-2014-a-chart/

Vendors' Middle Kingdoms

As chief architect of a large company you'll quickly gather new friends: account managers, (presales) solution architects, sales executives. Don't blame them – their job is to sell their products to large enterprises like yours, which rely heavily on external hardware, software, and services. Most enterprises shouldn't custom build systems that aren't a competitive differentiator: for them a better accounting system is as valuable as better electricity – it's important to have but it isn't going to give any competitive advantage. So just as you're unlikely to benefit from your own power plant, you should also abstain from building your own accounting system.

Enterprise vendors are also an important source of information, especially for architects. I quite enjoy some of the conversations with their senior technical staff. However, do keep in mind that the information you are given might be skewed by the vendor's world view. Most enterprise vendors live in their own *middle kingdom*, generally depicting their home state disproportionately large and allowing a fair degree of distortion on the periphery. I often joke that if you have no concept whatsoever of what a car is and only ever talked to one specific German automaker, you end up walking away with the firm belief that a star emblem on the hood is a defining feature of an automobile.

IT architects in large enterprises must therefore develop their own, balanced world view so they can safely navigate the treacherous waters of enterprise architecture and IT transformation. Vendors' distortion doesn't imply deception; it's largely a byproduct of the context people grew up in. If you develop databases, it's natural to view the database as the center of any application: after all that's where the data is stored. Server and storage hardware are viewed as parts of a *database appliance* while application logic becomes a *data feed*. Conversely, to a storage hardware manufacturer everything else is just "data", and databases are lumped into a generic "middleware" segment. It's like me on my first trip to Australia considering a quick hop to New Zealand because I thought it's so super-close. Realizing that it's still a good 3-and-a-half hour flight from Melbourne to Auckland proved that my world map is also distorted on the periphery.

Plotting Your World Map

To avoid falling into the "star on the hood" or the "it's all a database" trap, it's important that your architecture team first develops its own, undistorted map of the IT landscape - a great exercise for *Enterprise Architects* (4). Luckily, the world of IT is flat, so it's a bit easier to plot on a whiteboard or a piece of paper. Your own map gives you a much better, product-neutral understanding and may, for example, illustrate that a car's drive train is much more relevant than the hood emblem.

It's OK to draw the map piece-by-piece, starting, for example, where a new product needs to be placed. Drawing your map requires you to piece together distorted information from various sources, including vendors, blogs, or industry analyst reports. Resist the temptation to simply ask your favorite 2- or 3-lettered enterprise supplier to make the map for you. For one, it'll be distorted and today's rate of innovation outpaces most vendor product roadmaps, so it'll be outdated as well. Also, stay away from product names: IT architecture operates *between* the buzzword and the product names. Describing the architecture of a big data system as "Oracle" is no more useful than claiming the architecture of a house is "Ytong"[45]. Architecture is less concerned with the pieces, but with how they are put together. That's why it's so important to *not only look at the boxes, but also the lines* (22).

---

[45]Ytong is the name of a popular brand of aerated concrete bricks used for building construction in Europe.

A colleague of mine did a mapping exercise for application monitoring: black-box monitoring, white-box monitoring, troubleshooting, log analysis, alerting, and predictive monitoring all are distinct, but interrelated aspects of an application monitoring solution. Many vendors will also include performance testing as that's their heritage. Do you agree? Or is it part of the development tool chain? You decide!

Drawing the "borders" in your map means doing architecture in the enterprise! The word *reference architecture* even comes to mind even though I feel that most of them should have the disclaimer "Any similarities with real persons or systems is purely coincidental." printed at the bottom.

Ironically, conducting the worthwhile exercise of plotting your own IT world map can be challenged by traditional IT managers as "academic", which is especially amusing in Germany where IT management is littered with PhD's (not necessarily in any technical major) who carry the title "Dr." as a legal part of their name. If "pragmatic" means haphazard, I am happy to be in the "academic" camp: I am paid to think and plan, not to play product lottery.

Charting Territory

A vivid example of the difficulty of discussing product fit without a good map came up in a conversation about setting up a Web portal:

A local IT manager lamented the lack of documentation on port forwarding. When the solution architect replied that that's because the web server isn't part of the solution, much debate ensued. The local IT's port forwarding was implemented in a product from *F5*, which includes load balancing, reverse proxy, authentication, and much more. To them port forwarding doesn't have anything to do with a web server.

To resolve the mix-up, one needs to look at the map to get the proverbial "lay of the land". In this case, the best match is the concept of an *Application Delivery Controller* (ADC), which manages Web traffic, including functions like reverse proxying, load balancing, and port forwarding. You can utilize a web server as ADC in simple cases, or purchase an integrated product like *F5*. In the end the IT manager and the architect were talking about the same place on the map but confused each other with inconsistent vocabulary.

Product Philosophy Compatibility Check

Once I have a reference map, I like to understand whether a vendor's and our world view align. For that I prefer to meet with vendors' senior technical staff, such as a CTO, because too many "solution architects" are just glorified technical sales people. When the account manager starts the meeting with "please help us understand your environment", which roughly translates into "please tell me what I should sell to you", I typically preempt the exercise by asking the senior person about their product philosophy. Discussing what base assumptions and decisions are baked into a product gives great insight into a vendor's world map. Asking them about the toughest problem they had to solve when developing their product tells you much about where the center of their map is located. Naturally, this only works when talking to someone who is actually working on the product. Looking at the company leadership page or at the company history can also help you understand "where they come from".

When asking these questions to a monitoring vendor it became clear that a key benefit was being able to use the product without having access to the running application's source code. This is a very useful feature if you look at the problem from an operational point of view, especially if you work in an organization that *separates "change" from "run"* (12). However, in an environment where development teams are involved in operational aspects and have easy access to the source code, this intellectual property would be less valuable. You may end up paying for something that you don't need.

Such a comparison isn't about being right or wrong, it's about comparing world views. For example, I believe that a good programming language and a disciplined SDLC beats *"easy" configuration* (11). That's because I come from a software engineer mindset. Other folks may be happy to not have to hassle with `git stash` and compilation errors and prefer the vendor's configuration tools.

Once I am convinced that the product is "compatible" with our belief system, I am interested in seeing how it integrates into our landscape. I sometimes liken this exercise to playing Tetris. The "best" piece depends on what you have built up so far.

Shifting Territory

While the real world is relatively static (continental drift is pretty slow and the trend of splitting countries in the 90ies has also slowed down a bit), the world of IT is changing faster than ever. New technology trends also bring new buzzwords: will your app run in a container? Because it's difficult for a vendor to change its product philosophy, you will likely encounter old products with a new coat of paint on it. Your job as an architect is to look through the shiny new paint and see whether there's any rust or filler underneath.

Mapping Standards

Most large IT organizations *govern their product portfolio* (28)
via a standards group to reduce product diversity and to harvest
economies of scale, for example by bundling purchasing power.
They define a standard by filling a strategic need (or gap) with a
specific product selection. Essentially, they are placing products
on a neutral world map. The map will help you assess how well
a vendor's product fills it. Some products may not completely
cover the gap, while others have significant overlap with solutions
already in place. Yup, it's a bit like Tetris.

For example, if an organization wants to standardize database products, you'd need to first define whether you standardize relational
databases separately from NOSQL databases and, if so, whether
you want to distinguish between document and graph databases.
Basically, you need to decide whether it's one "country" or three.
Next, you'd need guidelines for which type of database is applicable
in which context. Only then should you look at products: before you
visit car dealers you should know whether you want a minivan or
a two-seater sports car. Or visit Porsche - they seem to be making
everything these days.

For storage, you need to distinguish SAN from NAS and differen-
tiate backup storage from direct attached storage. And you may be
looking into HDFS (Hadoop File System) and converged / so-called
"hyperconverged" storage (a storage virtualization layer over local
disks). Once your IT world map has undisputed borders, you can
start populating "countries" with products and avoid skirmishes.

14. Never Send a Human to Do a Machine's Job

Automate Everything. What you can't automate, make a self-service.

Sending a machine to do a human's job

Who would have thought that one can learn so much about large-scale IT architecture from the movie trilogy *The Matrix*? Acknowledging that the Matrix is run by machines, it should not be completely surprising to find some nuggets of system design wisdom, though: Agent Smith teaches us that one should never send a human to do a machine's job after his deal with Cypher, one of Morpheus' human crew members, to betray and hand over his boss failed.

Automate Everything!

There's a certain irony in the fact that corporate IT, which has largely established itself by automating business processes, is often not very automated itself. Early in my corporate career, I shocked a large assembly of infrastructure architects by declaring my strategy as: "automate everything and make those parts that can't be automated a self-service." The reaction ranged from confusion and disbelief to mild anger. Still, this is exactly what Amazon & Co. have done. And they have revolutionized how people procure and access IT infrastructure along the way. They have also attracted the top talent in the industry to build said infrastructure. If corporate IT wants to remain relevant, this is the way they ought to be thinking!

It's Not Only About Efficiency

Just like test-driven development is not a testing technique (it's primarily a design technique), automation is not just about efficiency, but primarily about repeatability and resilience. A vendor's architect once stated that automation shouldn't be implemented for infrequently performed tasks because it isn't economically viable. Basically, the vendor calculated that writing the automation would take more hours than would ever be spent completing the task manually (they also appeared to be on a fixed-price contract).

I challenged this reasoning with the argument of repeatability and traceability: wherever humans are involved, mistakes are bound to happen and work will be performed ad-hoc without proper documentation. That's why you don't send humans to do a machine's job. The error rate is actually likely to be the highest for infrequently performed tasks because the operators are lacking routine.

The second counter-example are disaster scenarios and outages: one hopes that they occur infrequently, but when they happen, the systems better be fully automated to make sure they can return to a running state as quickly as possible. The economic argument here isn't about saving manpower, but to minimize the loss of business during the outage, which far exceeds the manual labor cost. To appreciate this thinking, one needs to understand *Economies of Speed* (31). Otherwise, you may as well argue that the fire brigade should use a bucket chain because all those fire trucks and pumps are not economically viable given how rarely buildings actually catch fire.

Repeatability Grows Confidence

When I automate tasks, the biggest immediate benefit I usually derive is increased confidence. For example, when I wrote this book in Markdown to be rendered by leanpub.com, I had to maintain two slightly different versions: the e-book version uses hyperlinks for chapter references whereas the print version uses chapter numbers. After quickly becoming tired of manually converting between the formats, I developed two simple scripts that switch between print and e-pub versions of the text. Because it was easy to do, I also made the scripts idempotent, meaning that running a script multiple times causes no harm. With these scripts at hand, I didn't even worry a split second about switching between formats because I could be assured that nothing would go wrong. Automation is hugely liberating and hence speeds up work significantly.

Self-service

Once things are fully automated, users can directly execute common procedures in a self-service portal. To provide the necessary parameters, e.g. the size of a server, they must have a clear mental model of what they are ordering. Amazon Web Services provides a good example of an intuitive user interface, which not only alerts you that your server is reachable from any computer in the world, but even detects your IP address to restrict access. In a dramatic counter-example that used a spreadsheet as "user interface" for ordering a Linux server, I was told that I should just copy the network settings from an existing server because I wouldn't be able to understand what I need anyway. Designing good user interfaces can be a challenging but valuable exercise for infrastructure engineers who are largely used to working in hiding on rather esoteric "plumbing". It's also a chance for them to *show the Pirate Ship* (19), which is far more exciting than all the bits and pieces it's made out of.

Self-service doesn't at all imply that infrastructure changes become a free-for-all. Just like a self-service restaurant still has a cashier, validations and approvals apply to users' change requests. However, instead of a human re-coding a request submitted in free-form text or an Excel spreadsheet, the approval workflow simply pushes the requested change into production without further human intervention and possibility of error. Self-service also reduces input errors: because free-form text or an Excel spreadsheet rarely perform validations, input errors lead to lengthy e-mail cycles or pass through unnoticed. An automated approach gives immediate feedback to the user and makes sure the order actually reflects what the user needs.

Beyond Self-service

Configuration changes are best submitted into a source code repository where approvals can be handled via *pull requests* and *merge* operations, which trigger an automated deployment into production. Source code management has long known how to administer large volumes of complex changes through review and approval processes, including commenting and audit trails. We should leverage these processes for configuration changes so we can start to *think like a software developer* (15).

Most enterprise software vendors pitch graphical user interfaces as the ultimate in ease of use and cost reduction. However, in large-scale operations the opposite is the case: manual entry into user interfaces is cumbersome and error prone, especially for repeated requests or complex setups. If you need 10 servers with slight variations, would you want to enter this data 10 times by hand? Fully automated configurations should therefore be done via APIs, which can be integrated with other systems or scripted as part of higher-level automation.

Allowing users to specify what they want and providing it quickly in high quality would seem like a pretty happy scenario. However, in the digital world one can always push things a little further. For example, Google's "zero click search" initiative, which resulted in "Google Now", considered even one user click too much of a burden, especially on mobile devices. The system should anticipate the users' needs and answer before a question is even asked. It's like going to McDonalds and finding your favorite happy meal already waiting for you at the counter. Now that's customer service! An IT world equivalent may be auto-scaling, which allows the infrastructure to automatically provision additional capacity under high load situations without any human intervention.

Automation is Not a One-way Street

Automation usually focuses on the top-down part, e.g. configuring a piece of low-level equipment based on a customer order or the needs of a higher-level component. However, we will learn that *Control is an illusion* (23) wherever humans are involved, and that "control" necessitates two-way communication that includes an understanding of the current system state: when your room is too hot, you want the control system to turn on the air conditioning instead of the heater. The same is true in IT system automation: to define what hardware to order or what network changes to request, you likely first need to examine the current state. Therefore, full transparency on existing system structures and a clear vocabulary are paramount. In a recent example, it took us weeks just to understand whether a data center has sufficient spare capacity to deploy a new application. All order process automation doesn't help if it takes weeks to understand the current state of affairs.

Explicit Knowledge is Good Knowledge

Tacit knowledge is knowledge that exists only in employees' heads but isn't documented or encoded anywhere. Such undocumented knowledge can be a major overhead for large or rapidly growing organizations because it can easily be lost and requires new employees to re-learn things the organization already knew. Encoding tacit knowledge, which existed only in an operator's head, into a set of scripts, tools, or source code makes these processes visible and eases knowledge transfer. Tacit knowledge is also a sore spot for any regulatory body whose job it is to assure that businesses in regulated industries operate according to well-defined and repeatable principles and procedures. Full automation forces processes to be well-defined and explicit, eliminating unwritten rules and undesired variation inherent in manual processes. Ironically, classic IT often insists on manual steps in order to maintain separation of duty, ignoring the fact that approving a change and manually conducting a change are independent things.

A Place for Humans

If we automate everything, is there a place left for humans? Computers are much better at executing repetitive tasks, but while us humans are no longer unbeatable at the board game *Go*, we are still number one in coming up with new and creative ideas, designing things or automating stuff. We should stick to this separation of duty and let the machines do the repeatable tasks without fearing that Skynet will take over the world any moment.

15. If Software Eats the World, Better Use Version Control!

As your infrastructure becomes software-defined, you need to think like a software developer.

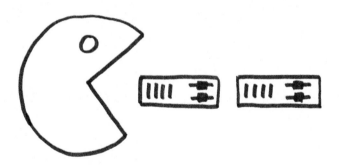

Software eats infrastructure

If software does indeed eat the world, it will have IT infrastructure for breakfast: the rapidly advancing virtualization of infrastructure from virtual machines and containers to so-called *lambda* and *serverless* architectures turns provisioning code onto a piece of hardware into a pure software problem. This is where Corporate IT's *uneasy relationship with code* (11) and lack of familiarity with the modern development lifecycle can be a dangerous proposition.

SDX - Software-defined Anything

Much of traditional IT infrastructure is either hard-wired or semi-manually configured: servers are racked and cabled, network switches are manually configured with tools or config files. Operations staff, who endearingly refer to their equipment as "metal", is usually quite happy with this state of affairs: it keeps the programmer types away from critical infrastructure where the last thing one needs is bugs and stuff like "agile" development, which is still *widely misinterpreted* (27) as doing random stuff and hoping for the best.

This is rapidly changing, though, and that's a good thing. The continuing virtualization of infrastructure makes resources that were once shipped by truck or wired by hand available via a call to an OpenStack API. It's like going from haggling in a car dealership and waiting four months for delivery just to find out that you should have ordered the premium seats after all to locating a Zipcar / DriveNow from your mobile phone and driving off three minutes later. Virtualized infrastructure is an essential element to keeping up with the scalability and evolution demands of digital applications. You can't run an agile business model when it takes you four weeks to get a server and four months to get it on the right network segment.

Operating-system-level virtualization is by no means a new invention, but the "software-defined" trend has extended to SDN, *Software-defined Networks*, and full-blown SDDC, *Software Defined Data Centers*. If that isn't enough, you can opt for *SDX* – Software Defined *Anything*, which includes virtualization of compute, storage, network and whatever else can be found in a data center, hopefully in some coordinated manner.

As so often, it's easy to look into the future of IT by reading Google's research papers that describe their systems of 5+ years ago (side note: finally there is an official paper on Borg[46], Google's

---

[46]http://static.googleusercontent.com/media/research.google.com/en//pubs/archive/43438.pdf

cluster manager). To get a glimpse of where SDN is headed, look at what Google has done with the so-called Jupiter Network Architecture[47]. If you are too busy to read the whole thing, this three-liner will do to get you excited: "Our latest-generation Jupiter network [...] delivering more than 1 Petabit/sec of total bisection bandwidth. This means that each of 100,000 servers can communicate with one another in an arbitrary pattern at 10Gb/s." This can only be achieved by having a network infrastructure that can be configured based on the applications' needs and is considered as an integral part of the overall infrastructure virtualization.

The Loomers' Riot?

New tools necessitate a new way of thinking, though, to be useful. It's the old "a fool with a tool is still a fool." I actually don't like this saying because you don't have to be a fool to be unfamiliar with a new tool and a new way of thinking. For example, many folks in infrastructure and operations are far detached from the way contemporary software development is done. This doesn't make them fools in any way, but it prevents them from migrating into the "software-defined" world. They may have never heard of unit tests, continuous integration, or build pipelines. They may have been led to believe that "agile" is a synonym for "haphazard" and also haven't had enough time to conclude that immutability is an essential property and that rebuilding / regenerating a component from scratch beats making incremental changes.

As a result, despite being the bottleneck in an IT ecosystem that demands ever faster changes and innovation cycles, operations teams are often not ready to hand over their domain to the "application folk" who can script the heck out of the software-defined anything. One could posit that such behavior is akin to the Loomer Riots because the economic benefits of a software-defined infrastructure

---

[47]http://googleresearch.blogspot.de/2015/08/pulling-back-curtain-on-googles-network.html

are too strong for anyone to put a stop to it. At the same time, it's important to get those folks on board that keep the lights on and understand the existing systems the best, so we can't ignore this dilemma.

Explaining to everyone What is Code?[48] is certainly a step in the right direction. As I often say: "if software eats the world, there will be only two kinds of people: those who tell the machines what to do and those where it's the other way around." Having more senior management role models who can code would be another good step. However, living successfully in a software-defined world isn't a simple matter of learning programming or scripting.

Think like a Software Developer!

A great example of having to think differently was provided when we explained the need for reversibility to a vendor: if a configuration isn't working, it needs to quickly revert to the last known stable state to minimize recovery time. With manual updates, this is very difficult and time-consuming at best, but in a software-defined and automated world it's much easier. The vendor countered that such a capability would require an explicit "undo" script for each possible action, rendering the automation very expensive and complex.

Their response highlights that many infrastructure teams don't quite yet think like software developers. Experienced software developers know that if their automated build system can build an artifact, such as a binary image or a piece of configuration, from scratch, they can easily revert to a previous version without having to undo anything. They reset version control to the last known good version, rebuild from scratch, and republish this "undone" configuration. Software build processes simply redo things instead of undoing because they embrace software being ephemeral. By making infrastructure software-defined, it can also become ephemeral. This is a huge shift in mindset, especially when you consider the annual

---

[48]http://www.bloomberg.com/graphics/2015-paul-ford-what-is-code/

depreciation cost of all that hardware, but only thinking this way can provide the true benefit of being software-defined.

In complex software projects rolling things back is a quite normal procedure, often instigated by the so-called "build cop" after failing automated tests cause the build to go "red". The build cop will ask the developer who checked in the offending code to make a quick fix or simply reverts that code submission. Configuration automation tools have a similar ability to regain a known stable state and can be applied to reverting and automatically re-configuring infrastructure configurations.

Use a Build Pipeline

Software-defined infrastructure shuns the notion of "snowflake" or "pet" servers, servers that have been running for a long time without a reinstall, have a unique configuration[49], and are manually maintained with great care. "This server has been up for 2 years" turns from bragging rights into a risk: who can recreate this server if it does go down? In a software-defined world, a server or network component can be reconfigured or re-created automatically with ease, similar to re-creating a Java build artefact. You no longer have to be afraid to mess up a server instance because it can easily be recreated via software in minutes.

Software-defined infrastructure therefore isn't just about replacing hardware configuration with software, but primarily about adopting a rigorous development lifecycle based on disciplined development, automated testing, and continuous integration. Over the last decades, software teams have learned how to move quickly while maintaining quality. Turning hardware problems into software problems allows you to take advantage of this body of knowledge.

---

[49]Just like every snowflake is unique, "snowflake servers" are those that don't match a standard configuration.

Automated Quality Checks

One of Google's critical infrastructure pieces was a router, which would direct incoming traffic to the correct type of service instance. For example, HTTP requests for maps.google.com would be forwarded to a service serving up maps data, as opposed to the search page. The router was configured via a file consisting of hundreds of regular expressions. Of course, this file was under version control as it should be.

 Despite rigorous code reviews invariably someday someone checked in a misconfiguration. It immediately brought down most of Google's services because the requests weren't routed to the corresponding service instance. Luckily, because the file was under version control, the previous version was quickly restored. Google's answer wasn't to disallow changes to this file as that would have slowed things down. Rather, automatic checks were added to the code submit pipeline to make sure that syntax errors or conflicting regular expressions are detected *before* the file is checked into the code repository.

When working with software-defined infrastructure you need to work like you would in professional software development.

Proper Language

One curiosity about Google is that no one working there ever used buzzwords like "Big data", "Cloud", or "Software-defined data center" because Google had all these things well before the buzzwords were created by industry analysts: much of Google's infrastructure was software-defined 10 years ago. When deploying many compute tasks into a data center, each process instance must be configured with small variations. For example, front-ends 1 through 4 may connect to back-end *A* while front-ends 5 to 7 connect to back-end *B*. Maintaining individual configuration files for each instance would be cumbersome and error-prone, especially as the system scales up and down. Instead, configurations are generated via a well-defined functional language called BCL, which supports templates, value inheritance, and built-in functions like map() that are convenient for manipulating lists of values.

While avoiding the *trap of configuration files* (11), learning a custom functional language to describe deployment descriptors may not be everyone's cup of tea. When configuration programs became more complex, causing testing and debugging configurations to become an issue, folks wrote an interactive expression evaluator and unit testing tools. That's what software people do to solve a problem: solve software problems with software!

The BCL example highlights what a real software-defined system looks like: well-defined languages and tooling that make infrastructure part of the software development lifecycle. Graphical user interfaces for infrastructure configuration, which vendors often like to show off, should be banned because they don't integrate well into a software lifecycle, aren't testable, and are error prone.

Software eats the world, one revision at a time

There's much more to being software-defined than a few scripts and config files. Rather, it's about making infrastructure part of your software development lifecycle (SDLC). First, make sure your SDLC is fast but disciplined and automated but quality-oriented. Second, apply the same thinking to your software-defined infrastructure. Or else you may end up with *SDA*, Software-Defined Armageddon.

Communication

Architects don't live in isolation. It's their job to gather information from disparate departments, articulate a cohesive strategy, communicate decisions, and win supporters at all levels of the organization. Communication skills are therefore paramount for architects. Conveying technical content to a diverse audience is challenging, though, because many classical presentation or writing techniques don't work well for highly technical subjects. For example, slides with single words superimposed on dramatic photographs may draw the audience's attention, but aren't particularly useful for a detailed explanation of your cloud computing platform strategy.

You can't manage what you can't understand

"You can't manage what you can't measure" is a common management slogan. However, for the measurements to be meaningful, you first have to understand the dynamics of the system you are managing. Otherwise you can't tell which levers you should pull to *influence the system behavior* (10).

Understanding what you are managing becomes an enormous challenge for decision makers in a world where technology invades all parts of personal and professional lives. While no business executive is expected to code a solution him- or herself, ignoring technological evolution and capabilities invariably leads to missed business opportunities or missed expectations when IT systems don't deliver what the business needs. Managing complex technology projects by timeline, staffing, and budget alone is no longer going to suffice in the digital world that demands *ever faster delivery of functionality at high quality* (36).

Architects must help close the gap between technical knowledge holders and high-level decision makers by clearly communicating the ramifications of technical decisions on the business, e.g. through development and operational cost, flexibility, or time-to-market. It's not only the "business types" who face challenges in understanding complex technology, though. Even architects and developers cannot possibly keep up with all aspects of intricate technical solutions, forcing them to also rely on easy-to-understand, but technically accurate descriptions of architectural decisions and their implications.

Getting Attention

Technical material can be very exciting, but ironically more so to the presenter than to the audience. Keeping attention through a lengthy presentation on code metrics or data center infrastructure can be taxing for even the most enthusiastic audience. Decision makers don't just want to see the hard facts, but also be engaged and motivated to support your proposal. Architects therefore have to use both halves of their brain to not only make the material logically coherent, but to also craft an engaging story.

Pushing Paper

The technical decision papers published by my team yielded much praise, but also unexpected criticism like "All that architects can do is produce paper". You might want to remind people that documentation provides value in numerous ways:

- *Coherence* - Agreeing on and documenting design principles and decisions improves consistency of decision making and thus preserves the conceptual integrity of the system design.

- *Validation* - Structured documentation can help identify gaps and inconsistencies in the design.
- *Clarity of Thought* - You can only write what you have understood. If someone claims that writing their thoughts down is too much effort, I routinely challenge them that this is likely because they haven't really understood things in the first place.
- *Education* - New team members become productive faster if they have access to good documentation.
- *History* - Some *decisions* (9) were good decisions at the time based on the context and what was known. Documentation can help understand what these were.
- *Stakeholder Communication* - Architecture documentation can help steer a diverse audience to the same level of understanding.

Useful documentation doesn't imply reams of paper, rather the opposite: most technical documents my team writes are subject to a five-page limit.

The Code is the Documentation?

Some developers claim that the source code is their documentation. They might be (mostly) right as long as all audience groups have access to the code, the code is understandable for all of them, and tools such as search are available. Generating diagrams and documentation from code are useful techniques. They struggle, though, in giving people the proverbial big picture and explaining why things were done the way they are because they generally fail to place the appropriate emphasis. Defining what is "interesting" or "noteworthy" largely remains a human task.

Choosing the Right Words

Technical writing is difficult, as evidenced by user manuals, which must rank as some of the most ridiculed pieces of literature, if we may even call them that. They may be surpassed in lack of empathy only by tax form instruction sheets. Architects must therefore be able to engage readers who wasted years of their career perusing poorly-written manuals and who may never want to read anything technical again outside of the occasional Dilbert comic. Careful choice of words and clean sentence structures go a long way towards assisting readers in grasping difficult concepts.

Communication Tools

This chapter examines some of the challenges of technical communication and gives advice on how to overcome them:

- Our stuff is complicated. Helping management reason about complex technical topics requires you to build a *careful ramp for the audience* (16).
- People are busy. They won't read every line you write, so make it easy for them to *navigate your documents* (17).
- There's always too much to tell. If everything is important, nothing is important. *Place an emphasis* (18)!
- Excite your audience by not just showing the building blocks, but also *the pirate ship* (19).
- Technical staff often struggles to create a good picture. Help them by *sketching bank robbers* (20).
- A picture can not only say more than a thousand words but actually *help you design better systems* (21).
- Your audience often understands the components, but not their relationships. You must *draw a line* (22).

16. Explaining Stuff

Build a ramp for the reader, not a cliff!

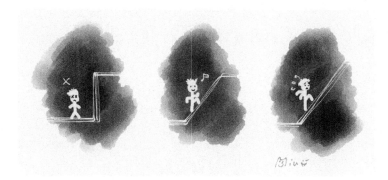

Build a ramp, not a cliff for the reader

Martin Fowler occasionally introduces himself as a guy "who is good at explaining things". While this certainly has a touch of British Understatement™, it also highlights a critically important but rare skill in IT. Too often technical people produce either an explanation at such a high level that it is almost meaningless or spew out reams of technical jargon with no apparent rhyme or reason.

High-performance Computing Architectures for Executives

A team of architects once presented a new hardware and software stack for high-performance computing to a management steering committee. The material covered everything from workload management down to storage hardware. It contrasted vertically integrated stacks like Hadoop and HDFS, which comprise a file system and a workload distribution mechanism, against stand-alone workload management solutions like LSF, which run on top of an independent high performance file system. In one of the comparison slides "POSIX compliance" jumped out as a selection criteria. While this may be completely appropriate, how do you explain to someone who knows little about file systems what this means, why it is important, and what the ramifications are?

Build a ramp, not a cliff

We often refer to learning curves as "steep", meaning it is tough for newcomers to become familiar with, or "ramp up" on, a new system or tool. I tend to assume my executive audience is quite intelligent (you don't get that high up simply by brown-nosing and playing politics), so they can in fact climb up a pretty steep learning ramp. What they cannot do is climb up a vertical cliff.

Building a logical sequence that enables the audience to draw conclusions in an unfamiliar domain can be "steep", but doable. Being bombarded with out-of-context acronyms or technical jargon constitutes a "cliff". "POSIX compliance" is a cliff for most people. You can turn it into a ramp by explaining that POSIX is a standard programming interface for file access, which is widely adhered to by Unix distributions, thus avoiding lock-in. Once you have built this ramp, executives can quickly reason that because they standardized on a single Linux distribution, POSIX compliance doesn't add much value as long as the file system is compatible with the standard distribution. It's also not relevant for vertically integrated systems like Hadoop, which include the file system. By building a ramp out of just a few words, you managed to involve someone who isn't deeply technical in the decision-making process. The ramp may not take the audience into the depths of POSIX versions and Linux flavors, but it provides a mental model to reason within the scope of the proposed decision.

A steep ramp is suitable for a quick climb, but becomes too tiresome if you are trying to lead your audience up Mt. Everest. Therefore, consider how high (or deep) your audience needs to go to reason about what is presented. When defining terms, define them within the context of your problem, highlighting the relevant properties and omitting irrelevant detail. For example, details about POSIX history and Linux Standard Base aren't pertinent to the decision above and should be omitted.

Mind the Gap

The ramp should not only provide a reasonable incline, but also avoid gaps or jumps in logic. Experts often don't perceive these gaps because their mind silently fills them in. This is a phenomenal feature of our brain, but an audience not intimately familiar with the topic is likely to stumble over even a minor gap and lose track of the line of reasoning.

 At a discussion about network security a team of architects presented their requirement that servers located in the untrusted network zone have separate network interfaces, so-called NICs, for incoming and outgoing network traffic to avoid a direct network path from the Internet to trusted systems. They continued with a statement that the vendor's "3 NIC design" cannot meet their requirement. To me, this made no sense: why is a server with three network interfaces unable to support a design requiring two interfaces, one for incoming traffic and one for outgoing? The answer was "obvious" to those who are familiar with the context: each server uses one additional network interface each for backup and management tasks, bringing the number of required ports to four, which clearly exceeds three. Skipping this detail created a gap large enough for the audience (and me) to stumble.

How big a gap they are creating is difficult to judge for the presenter. In the example above, just a few words or two additional labeled lines in the diagram would have been enough to bridge the gap. That, however, doesn't imply that the gap itself was small. The best way I have found to test for gaps is to present the line of reasoning to a person not familiar with the topic and to ask them to "teach back" what you explained to them, similar to holding a *Pop Quiz* (18).

First, create a language

When preparing technical conversations, I tend to use a two-step approach: first I set out to establish a basic mental model based on concrete vocabulary. Once equipped with this, the audience is able to reason in the problem space and to discern the relevance of parameters onto the decision. The mental model doesn't have to be anything formal, it merely has to give the audience a way to make a connection between the different elements that are being described.

In the file system example above I would first describe how file access is composed of a layered stack spanning from hardware (i.e. disk), basic block storage (like a SAN) to file systems and ultimately the operating system, which hosts the applications on top. This explanation doesn't even occupy half a slide and would nicely fit into a picture of layered blocks. Then I can use this vocabulary to explain that Hadoop is integrated from the application layer all the way down to the local file system and disks without any SAN, NAS or the like. This setup has specific advantages, such as low cost, data locality management etc., but requires you to build applications for this specific framework. In contrast, stand-alone file systems for high-performance computing, for example GPFS or pNFS, either build on top of standard file systems or provide "adapters" that make the proprietary file system available through widespread APIs, such as POSIX. You depict this in a diagram by having the Hadoop "stack" reach all the way from top to bottom while other systems provide "seams", including POSIX compliance. The audience can now easily understand why the POSIX feature is important, but Hadoop HDFS doesn't need to provide it.

Consistent level of detail

Determining the appropriate level of detail to support the line of reasoning is difficult. For example, we pretended "POSIX" is a single thing when in reality there are many different version and components, the Linux Standard Base etc. The ability to draw the line at roughly the right level of detail is an important skill of an architect. Many developers or IT specialists love to inundate their audience with irrelevant jargon. Others consider it all terribly obvious and leave giant gaps by omitting critical details. As so often, the middle ground is where you want to be.

Drawing the line at the right level of detail depends on you knowing your audience. If your audience is mixed, building a good ramp is ever more important as it allows you to catch up folks less familiar with the details without boring the ones who are. The highest form is building a ramp that audience members already familiar with the subject matter appreciate despite not having learned anything new. This is tough to achieve, but a noble goal to aim for.

Getting the level of detail "just right" is usually a crapshoot, even if you do know the audience. At least as important, though, is sticking to a consistent level of detail. If you describe high-level file systems on slide one and then dive into bit encoding on magnetic disks in slide two, you are almost guaranteed to either bore or lose your audience. Therefore, strive to find a line that maintains cohesion for reasoning about the architectural decision at hand, without leaving too many "dangling" aspects. Algorithm-minded people would phrase this challenge as a graph partition problem: your topic consists of many elements that are logically connected, just like a graph of nodes connected by edges. Your task is to split the graph, i.e. to cover only a subset of the elements, while minimizing the number of edges, i.e. logical connections, being cut.

I would have wanted to have liked to, but I didn't dare be allowed to

This poor translation of Karl Valentin's famous quote "Mögen hätt' ich schon wollen, aber dürfen habe ich mich nicht getraut" reminds me of the biggest challenge in explaining technical matter: too many architects believe their audience will never "get" their explanations, anyway. Some are also afraid that presenting technical detail will make them appear unfit for management. Others go a step further and actually prefer to confuse management with disconnected jargon so that their "decisions" (often simply preferences or vendor recommendations) aren't unnecessarily put into question by the audience.

I have a very critical view of such behavior. Your role as an architect is to get a broad audience to understand the ramifications of decisions and assumptions that were made. After all, this is where most of the biggest problems pop up. For example, if a few years down the road an IT system can no longer serve the business needs, it is often due to a constraint or an invalid assumption that was made but never clearly communicated. Communicating decisions and explaining trade-offs clearly protects both you and the business.

17. Writing for Busy People

Don't expect everyone to read word-by-word.

If you don't have time to read, look at the pictures.

Writing Scales

In large organizations communication across a large audience is critically important. I often prefer to do so in brief, but accurate technical position and decision papers, which have become a trademark of our architecture group. Writing is a tough business, though, because it takes so much more effort than reading. Still, the written word has distinct advantages over the spoken word:

1. it scales: you can address a large audience without gathering everyone in one room (podcasts admittedly can also accomplish that)
2. it's fast: people read 2-3 times faster than they can listen

3. it's searchable: you can find what you want to read quickly
4. it can be edited and versioned: everybody sees the same, versioned content

Consequently, writing pays off once you have a large (or important) enough audience. The biggest benefit, though, is Richard Guindon's insight that "Writing is nature's way of telling us how sloppy our thinking is." That alone makes writing a worthwhile exercise as it requires us to sort out our thoughts so we can put them into a somewhat cohesive storyline. Unlike most slide decks, well-written documents are also self-contained, so they can be widely distributed without further commentary.

While the title is a pun on the popular books "Japanese for busy People", it intentionally implies an ambiguity that we are both writing for a busy audience, but are busy authors as well.

Quality vs. Impact

The catch with writing is that while you can to some extent force people to (at least pretend to) listen to you, it's much harder to force anyone to read your text. I remind writers that "the reader is by no means required to turn the page. He or she decides based on what they read so far." Assuming the topic is interesting and relevant to the readership, I have repeatedly observed a non-linear relationship between the quality of the writing / editing and the actual readership, which is a good proxy metric for the impact of a technical paper: if the paper doesn't meet a minimum quality bar, e.g. it is verbose, poorly structured, full of typos, or displayed in some ridiculous, difficult to read font, people won't read it at all, resulting in zero impact. I call this the "trash bin" zone, named after the likely reader reaction. At the other end of the spectrum, additional impact from quality improvement quickly tapers off as the document approaches the "gold plating" zone.

So you want to get the quality of your writing into the "sweet spot" and then focus on content. While the sweet spot depends on the topic and the audience, I posit that it starts further to the right than most authors believe. Key influencers are very busy people and tend to shy away from anything that is more than a few pages long, unless it is from a high-paid consultancy, in which case they make someone else read it because they paid so much money for it. For this impatient readership, clarity of wording and brevity aren't nice-to-haves: a lack thereof will quickly put your paper quite literally into the "trash bin" zone. Blatant typos or grammar issues are like the proverbial fly in the soup: the taste is arguably the same, but the customer is unlikely to come back for more.

"In the hand" - First Impressions Count

When Bobby and I wrote "Enterprise Integration Patterns", the publisher highlighted the importance of the "in the hand" moment, which occurs when a potential buyer picks the book from the shelf to give a quick glimpse to front and back cover, maybe the table of contents, and to leaf through (back in 2003 people still bought books in physical bookstores). The reader makes the purchasing decision at this very moment, not when he or she stumbles on your ingenious conclusion on page 326. This is one reason why we included many diagrams in that book: almost all facing pages contain a graphical element, such as an icon (aka "Gregorgram"), a pattern sketch, a screen shot, or a UML diagram, sending the message to potential readers that it isn't an academic book, but a pragmatic and approachable one. Technical papers should do the same: use a clean layout, insert a handful of expressive diagrams, and, above all, keep it short and to the point!

To assess what a short paper will "feel" like to the reader without wasting printer paper, I zoom out my wysiwyg editor far enough that all pages appear on the screen. I can't read the text anymore, but can see the headings, diagrams, and overall flow, e.g. the length of paragraphs and sections. This is exactly how a reader will see it when flipping through your document to decide whether it's worth reading. If they see an endless parade of bullet points, bulky paragraphs, or a giant mess, the paper will leave "the hand" quite quickly as gravity teleports it into the recycling bin.

A good paper is like the movie "Shrek"

Most animated movies have to entertain multiple audiences: the kids who love the cute characters plus the adults who had to shell out thirty bucks to take the family to the movies and spend two hours watching cute characters. Great animated movies like *Shrek* manage to address both audiences by including humor for kids *and* adults. The audiences may laugh at slightly different scenes, but aren't distracted by each other. Technical papers that address a diverse audience should supply technical detail while also highlighting important decisions and recommendations. A few mechanisms can make reading your paper more like watching Shrek:

- *Story-telling headings* replace an executive summary: your reader should get the gist of the paper just by reading the headings. Such headings reduce word count and still take busy readers through the whole paper. Headings like "introduction" or "conclusion" aren't story-telling and have no place in a short paper.
- *Diagrams* provide a visual anchor for important sections. Readers who flip through a paper likely pause at a diagram, so it's good to position them strategically near critical sections.
- *Callouts*, i.e. short sections that are offset in a different font or color, indicate to the reader that this additional detail can be safely skipped without losing the train of thought.

Making it easy for the Reader

After a positive first impression, your readers will start reading your paper. For advice on technical writing, I recommend the book *Technical Writing and Professional Communication for Non-Native Speakers*[50], which sadly appears out of print, but is available used. It covers a lot of ground in its 700 pages, including authoring different types of documents, such as resumes. I find the sections towards the end on parallelism and paragraph structure most helpful. Parallelism demands that all entries in a list follow the same grammatical structure, e.g. all start with a verb or an adjective. A counter example would be:

System A is preferred because:

- *It's faster*
- *Flexibility*
- *We want to reduce cost*
- *Stable*
- *Don't forget to look at long-term evolution*

Such writing uses too many of your reader's brain cells just to parse the text instead of focusing on your message. Taking the "noise" out of the language reduces friction and allows your reader to focus on the content. Parallelism is not only useful in lists but also in sentences, e.g. when drawing analogies or contrasting.

Each paragraph should focus on a single topic and introduce that topic right at the beginning, like this very paragraph: readers can glean from the first few words that this paragraph is about paragraphs. They can also rest assured that I don't start talking about lists halfway through, so if they already know how to write a good paragraph, they can safely skip this one. That's why "It is further important to note that in some circumstances one has to pay special attention to..." makes for a very poor paragraph opening.

[50]Huckin; Olsen: Technical Writing and Professional Communication: For Nonnative Speakers of English, McGraw-Hill, 1991

The curse of writing: linearity

Technical topics are rarely one-dimensional, but your text is forced to be: one word after the other, one paragraph after the next. Only a well-thought-out logical structure can overcome this limitation, as described by Barbara Minto in her book *The Pyramid Principle*[51]. The "pyramid" in this context denotes the hierarchy of content, not the *Pyramids in IT* (24). While somewhat over-hyped and over-priced, the book's sections on order are a gem: every list or grouping should have an order, either by time (chronological), structure (relationships), or ranking (importance). Note that "alphabetical" and "serendipitous" aren't valid choices. "How is this ordered?" has become a standard question I ask when reviewing documents containing a list or grouping.

Loose usage of the word "this" as a stand-alone reference is another pet peeve of mine, e.g. stating that "this is a problem" without being clear what "this" actually refers to. Jeff Ullman cites such a "non-referential this" as one of the major impediments to clear writing, exemplified in his canonical example:

> If you turn the sproggle left, it will jam, and the glorp will not be able to move. This is why we foo the bar.[52]

Do we foo the bar because the glorb doesn't move or because the sproggle jammed? Programmers understand the dangers of dangling pointers and *Null Pointer Exceptions* well, but don't seem to apply the same rigor to writing – maybe because your readers don't throw a stack trace at you?

Another fantastic advice from Minto is the following:

> Making a statement to a reader that tells him something he doesn't know will automatically raise a logical ques-

---

[51]Minto, Barbara: The Pyramid Principle: Logic in Writing and Thinking, Prentice Hall, 2010
[52]Ullman, Jeff: Viewpoint: Advising students for success, Communications of the ACM, Vol. 52 Issue 3, March 2009

tion in his mind [...] the writer is now obliged to answer that question. The way to ensure total reader attention, therefore, is to refrain from raising any questions in the reader's mind before you are ready to answer them.

Follow this single piece of advice and your technical paper will stand above 80% of the rest. This rule also applies to unsubstantiated claims. An internal presentation once stated on the first slide: "only technology ABCD has proven to be a viable solution". When I demanded to see proof, it turned out that none existed due to "lack of time and funding." These aren't just wording issues, but fatal flaws. A reader no longer wants to see page 2 if they cannot trust page 1.

In der Kürze liegt die Würze[53]

In technical writing, your readers are not out to appreciate your literary creativity, but to understand what you are saying. Therefore, less is more when it comes to word count. While Walker Royce[54] spends a good part of his book musing about English words, his advice on brevity and editing is sound. His citation from Zinsser[55] on the usage of "I might add," "It should be pointed out," and "It is interesting to note." hits the mark: if you might add, add it. If it should be pointed out, point it out. If it is interesting to note, make it interesting. Royce also gives many concrete suggestions on how to replace long-winded expressions or "big" words with single, simple words, thereby not only reducing noise but also aiding non-native speakers.

If you are up to a more rigorous evaluation of properly linking words into sentences, and you are willing to put up with a few

---

[53]literally "brevity gives spice" ironically translating into "short and sweet"
[54]Royce, Walker: Eureka!: Discover and Enjoy the Hidden Power of the English Language, Morgan James Publishing, 2011
[55]Zinsser, William: On Writing Well: The Classic Guide to Writing Nonfiction, Harper, 2006

tirades and snipes, I recommend Barzun's *Simple & Direct*[56], which isn't simple, but pedantically direct.

Our team's internal editing cycles routinely cut word count by 20-30% despite including additional material or detail. To the first-time author this may be shocking, but Saint-Exupéry's adage that "perfection is achieved not when there is nothing more to add, but when nothing is left to take away" is especially true for technical papers (and good code for that matter). I actually just edited this very chapter down by 15%.

When this type of cruel editing was first bestowed upon me by a professional copy editor I felt that the document no longer sounded "like me". Over the years I have come to appreciate that being crisp and accurate is a great way to have a technical paper sound like me. Longer, more personal pieces like this book allow some "slack" to help the reader keep attention after many pages.

Writer's workshop

The most effective vehicle for improving technical papers is to hold a *writer's workshop*[57], which has people read and discuss a paper while the author is allowed to listen, but not to speak. This setup simulates a group of persons reading and discussing a paper, which also validates that the paper is self-contained. The author must remain silent because they cannot pop out of their paper to explain to each reader what was really meant. Because writer's workshops are time-intensive, they are best applied after the paper has gone through an initial review.

---

[56]Barzun, Jacques: Simple & Direct, Harper Perennial, 2001
[57]Gabriel, Richard P.: Writers' Workshops & the Work of Making Things, Pearson Education, 2002

The pen is mightier than the sword. But not mightier than corporate politics.

Producing high-quality position papers can lead to an unexpected amount of organizational head-wind. The word "perfection" is invariably used with a negative connotation by those who are poor writers or want to avoid sharing their team's work. Ironically, these are often the same departments that love to be entertained by colorful vendor presentations.

Other teams claim that their "agile" approach spares them from any need to produce documentation, notwithstanding the fact that those teams have no running code to show either. Agile software development places the emphasis on producing working code that is worth reading, but multi-year IT strategy plans are unlikely to manifest themselves in code alone. Alas, good documents seem to be even more difficult to find than good code.

Some corporate denizens actively resent writing clear and self-contained documents because they prefer to "tune" their story for each audience. Naturally, this approach *doesn't scale* (26).

Writing good documents in an organization that is generally poor at writing can give you significant visibility, but it can also rock the political system. The first time I sent a positioning paper on digital ecosystems to senior management, a person complained to both my boss and my boss's boss about me not having "aligned" the paper with her. Communication is a mighty tool and some people in your organization will fight hard to control it. Pick your targets wisely and make sure you have enough "ammunition".

18. Emphasis over Completeness

Show the forest, not the trees.

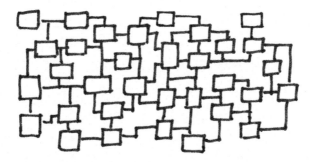

Can you spot the performance bottleneck in this database schema?

When I create a document or a diagram, feedback sometimes includes "ABC is missing" or "you could also include DEF". While this is well intentioned, I remind the reviewers that completeness wasn't my primary goal. Rather, I am looking for a scope that is big enough to be meaningful, small enough to be comprehensible, and cohesive enough to make sense. Compare this to drawing a map: a street map of Chicago that ends half-way through the city would be awkward. However, including all of Lake Michigan because the lake doesn't actually end in a straight line 3cm off the coastline would make the map a lot less useful. Adding Springfield at the same scale is also unlikely to be helpful.

Any diagram or text you create is a *model of reality* (21) that must set a specific emphasis to be useful. Comments like "ABC is missing" can be helpful to "round off" your model and make it more cohesive. But you also need to decide when something is better placed into another model. For me personally, I can make that decision really only once I have it in front of my eyes - it's not something I can do *a priori*.

A different kind of comment I tend to get is along the lines of "XYZ is another important problem". This is in fact frequent enough that my snip answer tends to be: "yes, there are children starving in India, too. But for now I am solving hunger in Africa". Especially in large organizations there's a constant danger of being diluted by the size and complexity in the environment, so putting some blinders on is allowed, and in fact necessary, to make an impact.

The 3-second Test

Short, technical documents, diagrams, or slide decks are designed to get a specific point across and therefore have to place a clear emphasis. They are different from a book or a manual, which has to be comprehensive. When dealing with overly "noisy" slides, a tough but useful test is the *3-second test*:

> I show the audience a slide for a mere 3 seconds and ask them to describe what they saw. In most cases, the responses boil down to a few words from the headline and statements like "2 yellow boxes on the left and one blue barrel on top". The authors are usually disappointed to hear this dramatic simplification of their precious content, but understand that less is indeed more.

Slides that don't pass this test are almost guaranteed to confuse the audience when they are first shown: viewers' eyes will chase across the visuals, trying to discern what's important and what's the meaning of it all. During that time your audience isn't listening to you explaining the content because they're busy with the visuals. Of course, you will show the final slide for more than 3 seconds, but first impressions count – for every slide you show.

Sometimes, architects have to show complex interrelationships in order to explain a particular *system behavior* (10). While opinions differ, I am fine to use a *build slide* or *incremental reveal* for this purpose because it allows me to explain one piece at a time.

Making a Statement

The slide or paragraph title sets the tone for a clear and focused statement. Some authors prefer titles that are full sentences while others prefer short phrases. After having gone back-and-forth throughout my career I settled on using both, but in different contexts: "big" presentations tend to have titles consisting of single words or short phrases like the *Architect Elevator* (2) because they represent a concept that I will explain. The visuals in this case are truly a *visual aid* to me, the speaker, to draw the audience's attention and help them memorize the content via a visual metaphor.

For technical presentations that are prepared for a review or decision-making session, however, I prefer clear statements, with which one can either agree or disagree. These statements are much better represented as full sentences, akin to the *story-telling headings* (17) in documents for busy people. In such cases, "Stateless application servers and full automation enable elastic scale-out" is a better title than "Server Architecture". What you certainly want to avoid are verbose phrases or crippled sentences that don't make a statement: "Server infrastructure and application architecture overview diagram (abstracted for simplicity's sake)."

A Pop Quiz

I participate in many architecture reviews and decision boards. While such boards often exist due to an undesirable *separation of decision-makers and knowledge holders* (2), many large enterprises need them to harmonize the technical landscape and to gain an overview across silos. The topics for these meetings can be fairly technical in nature, making me skeptical whether the audience is truly following along.

To ensure that the decision body understands what they are deciding, I inject a *pop quiz*[58] into the presentation by telling the presenter to pause and blank the slide (hitting "B" will do this in PowerPoint) and asking the audience who would like to recap what was said up to this point. After observing nervous laughter and frantic staring at the floor, I usually ask the presenter to try to recap the key points so we have a chance of passing this (fictitious) test. In the end, this is a test for the presenter more so than for the audience.

Simple Language

I don't exclude myself from the pop quiz. When replaying what the speaker said, I often intentionally use very simple language to make sure I really capture the essence. In a presentation about network security architecture in the untrusted network zone, after watching a handful of rather busy slides, I summarized the speaker's statement as follows: "what worries you is the black line going all the way from top to bottom?" His resounding "yes" both confirmed that I had correctly summarized the issue, and that the presenter took away insight how to better communicate this very aspect. While this technique may seem overly simplistic at first, it validates that there is a solid connection between the model being presented (such as vertical lines depicting legal network paths from the Internet to the trusted network) and the problem statement (security risks). Removing all noise and reducing the statement down to the "black line" sharpens the message.

---

[58]A pop quiz is a short test given by a teacher in class without prior announcement. It goes without saying that this is fairly unpopular with students.

Technical Memos

The idea to create documents that don't try to be encyclopedic (who reads an encyclopedia, anyway?), but describe a particular aspect of the system and place a specific emphasis on it, isn't new: 20 years ago, Ward Cunningham defined the notion of a *technical memo* in his *Episodes* pattern language[59]:

> Maintain a series of well formatted technical memoranda addressing subjects not easily expressed in the program under development. Focus each memo on a single subject. [...] Traditional, comprehensive design documentation [...] rarely shines except in isolated spots. Elevate those spots in technical memos and forget about the rest.

Keep in mind, though, that writing technical memos is more useful, but not necessarily easier than producing reams of mediocre documentation. The classic example of the concept of technical memos gone wrong is a project Wiki full of random, mostly outdated, and incohesive documentation. This isn't tool's fault (the Wiki was not quite coincidentally also invented by Ward), but rather due to a lack of emphasis being placed by the writers.

---

[59]Vlissides, Coplien, Kerth: Pattern Languages of Program Design 2, Addison-Wesley, 1996

19. Show the Kids the Pirate Ship!

Why the whole is much more than the parts.

This is what people want to see.

When you look at the cover of a Lego™ toy box you don't see a picture of each individual brick that's inside. Instead, you see the picture of an exciting, fully assembled model, such as a pirate ship. To make it even more exciting, the model isn't sitting on a living room table, but is positioned in a life-like pirate's bay with cliffs and sharks – captain Jack Sparrow would be jealous. What does this have to do with communicating system architecture and design? Sadly, not much, but it should! Technical communication too frequently makes the mistake of listing all the individual elements, but forgets to show the pirate ship: we see tons of boxes (and hopefully some *lines* (22)), but the *gestalt* of what they mean as a whole isn't clear.

Is this a fair comparison, though? Lego is selling toys to kids while architects need to explain the complex interplay between components to management and other professionals. Furthermore, IT professionals have to explain issues like network outages due to flooded network segments, something much less fun than playing pirates. I'd posit that we can learn quite a few things from the pirate ship for the presentation of IT architecture.

Get Attention

The initial purpose of the pirate ship is to draw attention among all the other competing toy boxes. While kids come to the toy store to hunt for new and shiny toys, many corporate meeting attendees are there because they were delegated by their boss, not because they want to hear your content. Grabbing their attention and getting them to put down their smartphones requires you to show something exciting. Sadly, many presentations start with a table of contents, which I consider extremely silly. First, it isn't exciting: it's like a list of assembly instructions instead of the ship. Second, a table of contents' purpose is to allow a reader to navigate a book or a magazine. If the audience has to sit through the whole presentation anyhow, there is no point in giving them a table of contents at the beginning. The old adage of "tell them what you are going to tell them", which is vaguely attributed to Aristotle, certainly doesn't translate into a slide with a table of contents. You are going to tell them how to build a pirate ship!

Excitement

Once children and your audience look at the pirate ship, they should feel excitement. How cool is this? There's sharks and pirates, daggers and cannons, chests of gold, and the parrot. You can feel the story unravel in your head just as you are reading the list of play pieces. Why should Platform-as-a-Service, API Gateways, Web Application Firewalls, and Build Pipelines tell a less exciting story? It's a story of gaining speed in the digital world where automated tests and build pipelines assure you good code quality despite fast pace, automated deployments bring repeatability, and Platform-as-a-Service provides elastic scalability. That's at least as exciting as a pirate story!

I am convinced that IT architecture can be much more exciting and interesting than people often believe. In an interview[60] with my Japanese friend Yuji back in 2004 I explained that software development is quite a bit more exciting than it appears on the outside – it is as exciting as you make it. If you regard software development as a pile of Legos, then you haven't seen the pirate ship! People who find software and architecture boring or just a necessary tedium haven't scratched the surface of software design and architecture thinking. They also haven't understood that IT isn't any longer a means to an end but an innovation driver for the business. They consider IT as randomly stacking Lego bricks when in reality we are building exciting pirate ships!

You may feel that excitement is a bit too frivolous for a serious workplace discussion. That's where you should look back at Aristotle. Some 2300 years ago he concluded that a good argument is based on *logos*, facts and reasoning, *ethos*, trust and authority, and *pathos*, emotion! Most technical presentations deliver 90% logos, 9% ethos, and maybe 1% pathos. From that starting point, a good dose of pathos can go a long way. You just have to make sure that your content can match the picture presented on the cover: pitching a

---

[60]https://www.ogis-ri.co.jp/otc/hiroba/specials/GregorHohpe/interview_2.html

pirate ship and not having the cannons inside the box is prone to lead to disappointment.

Focus on Purpose

Coming back to the pirate ship, the box also clearly shows the purpose of the pieces inside. The purpose isn't for the bricks to be randomly stacked together, but to build a cohesive, balanced solution. The whole really is much more than the sum of the parts in this case. It's the same with system design: a database and a few servers are nothing special, but a scale-out, masterless NoSQL database is quite exciting.

Alas, the technical staff who had to put all the pieces together is prone to dwell on said pieces instead of drawing attention to the purpose of the solution they built. They feel the audience has to appreciate the work that went into assembling the pieces as opposed to the usefulness of the complete solution. The bad news is: no one is interested in how much work it took you; people want to see the results you achieved.

Show Context

The Lego box cover image also shows the pirate ship within a useful context, such as a (fake) pirate's bay. Likewise, the context in which an IT system is embedded is at least as relevant as the intricacies of the internal design. Hardly any system lives in isolation and the interplay between systems is often more difficult to engineer than the innards of a single system. So you should show a system in its natural habitat.

Many architecture methods begin with a *system context diagram*, which rarely turns out to be a useful communication tool because it aims for a complete system specification without *Placing an Emphasis* (18). Such diagrams show a bunch of bricks, but not the pirate ship. They are therefore rarely suitable to be shown on the cover.

The Content on the Inside

Lego toys also show the exact part count and their assembly, but on a leaflet inside the box, not on the cover. Correspondingly, technical communication should display the pirate ship on the first page or slide and keep the description of the bricks and how to stack them together for the subsequent pages. Get your audience's attention, then take them through the details. If you do it the other way around, they may all be asleep by the time the exciting part finally comes.

Consider the Audience

Just like Lego has different product ranges for different age groups, not every IT audience is suitable for the pirate ship. To some levels of management that are far removed from technology you may need to show the little duckie made from a handful of Lego Duplo bricks.

Play at Work

While on the topic of toys: building pirate ships would be classified by most people as playing, something that is commonly seen as the opposite of work, as we are reminded by the proverb "all work and no play makes Jack a dull boy." Pulling another reference from the 80s movie archives, let's hope that lack of play doesn't have the same effect on IT architects as it had on the author Jack in the movie *The Shining* – he went insane and tried to kill his family. But it certainly stifles learning and innovation.

Most of what we know we didn't learn from our school teachers, but from playing and experimenting. Sadly, most people seem to have forgotten how to play, or were told not to, when they entered their professional life. This happens due to social norms, pressure to always be (or appear) productive, and fear. Playing knows no fear and no judgment; that's why it gives you an open mind for new things.

If playing is learning, times of rapid change that require us to learn new technologies and adapt to new ways of working should re-emphasize the importance of playing. I actively encourage engineers and architects in my team to play. Interestingly, Lego offers a successful method called *Serious Play*[61] for executives to improve group problem solving. They might be building pirate ships.

---

[61]http://www.seriousplay.com

20. Sketching Bank Robbers

Architects as police sketch artists

That's what he looked like!

With a demanding job like that of an architect in a large IT organization, it's a good exercise to do more of those things you enjoy and fewer of those you don't enjoy. Of course, this requires you to know what you truly enjoy (and truly despise) in the first place - an exercise that can be a little more challenging than it sounds, especially for left-brained IT architects. The latter is generally more easily answered: in my case it's 8am meetings with no particular objective that end up in a monologue of the highest-paid person. The former usually takes a bit more reflection. Over the years I have realized that one of my favorite work activities is to listen to system owners or solution architects describe their system, often in fragments, and to draw a cohesive picture for them. The most satisfying moment happens when they exclaim "that's exactly what it looks like" without them having been able to draw the picture themselves. This exercise is also a great opportunity to learn about those system details that aren't documented anywhere.

Asking people to tell you about their system so you can draw it for them may remind you of the old joke that describes *consultants* (1) as those people who borrow your watch to tell you what time it is (and charge you a lot of money for it). Drawing expressive architecture diagrams, though, is a bit more involved than reading the time off a watch. It extracts people's knowledge and presents it in a way that they weren't able to create themselves.

Being able to build a system doesn't automatically mean the same person is gifted at representing it in an intuitive way. Therefore, helping such a person draw a picture of their system can be quite valuable. I liken this task that of a police sketch artist.

Everyone saw the perpetrator

If a bank is robbed and you ask those people who saw the perpetrator to draw a picture, you'll likely end up with stick figures or very rough sketches. In any case, you won't get anything particularly useful even though the witnesses have a first-hand account of the person. Knowing something, being able to articulate it, and being able to draw it are three very different skills.

That's why a professional police sketch artist is usually brought in. The artist interviews the witnesses, asking them a series of questions that they can easily answer, such as "was the person tall?". Based on the descriptions the artist draws the picture, frequently obtaining feedback from the witnesses. After initially giving trivial facts like "he was tall", people end up confirming, "he looked just like that!"

A Police Sketch Artist

A police sketch artist is a fairly specialized job whose education includes both art and human anatomy. For example, a police sketch artist will undergo training in dental and bone structure as they influence the appearance of the suspect. The same is true for *architecture artists*: they need to have a minimum level of artistic skill, probably not quite at the level of the criminal sketch artist, but must also have the mental model and visual vocabulary to express architectural concepts.

Interestingly, sketch artists break down the problem and work with well-known "patterns": after initially asking very broad questions like "tell me about the person", the artist will guide the witness with typical patterns, for example, ethnicity or defining features, such as nose, eyes, or hair. To exaggerate, they won't discover that the person had two ears, two eyes, and one nose (if they don't, that's certainly worth mentioning!), but drive towards discriminating and defining features, just like we do when we try to tell whether *something is architecture* (9). In the world of IT, one would do the equivalent. For example, when looking at data storage we'd ask if there is an RDBMS or a NoSQL DB, perhaps a combination, caching, replication, etc.

When assuming the role of an "architecture sketch artist", I tend to pursue two different approaches, often sequenced one after the other.

The System Metaphor

First, I look for noteworthy or defining features, i.e. for the *key decisions* (9). Is it a pretty vanilla web-site for a customer to review information, like a *customer information portal*? Or is it rather a new sales channel, or even a piece of a cross-channel strategy? Is it designed to handle tons of volume or is it rather an experiment that will see little traffic, but must evolve very quickly? Or is it a spike to test out new technologies and the use case is secondary? Once I have established this frame, I start filling in the detail.

I am a big fan of Kent Beck's notion of a system metaphor that describes what kind of "thing" the system is. As Kent wisely states in *Extreme Programming Explained*[62]:

> We need to emphasize the goal of architecture, which is to give everyone a coherent story within which to work, a story that can easily be shared by the business and technical folks. By asking for a metaphor we are likely to get an architecture that is easy to communicate and elaborate.

In the same book Kent also states that "Architecture is just as important in XP [Extreme Programming] projects as it is in any software project", something to be kept in mind by folks who are tempted to shun architecture *because they are agile* (27).

Just like with *Diagram-driven Design* (21), architecture sketching can also be a useful design technique. If the picture makes no sense (and the architecture sketch artist is talented) then something may be inconsistent or wrong in the architecture.

Viewpoints

Once I have a rough idea about the nature of the system, I let the metaphor drive which aspects or viewpoints to examine. This is where doing an *architecture sketch* differs from performing an *architecture analysis*. An analysis typically walks through a fixed, structured set of aspects, as defined for example by methods such as ATAM[63] or arc42[64]. This is useful as a "checklist" to uncover missing aspects or gaps. In contrast, a criminal sketch artist doesn't want to

---

[62]Beck: Extreme Programming explained, Addison Wesley, 1999
[63]http://www.sei.cmu.edu/architecture/tools/evaluate/atam.cfm
[64]http://arc42.org/

draw the details of a person's trouser finishings (hemmed?, cuffed?), but highlight those characteristics that are unique or noteworthy. The same is true for the architecture sketch artist.

Following a fixed set of viewpoints always runs the risk of becoming a *Paint by Numbers* exercise where one fills in every section of a template, but forgets to *place an emphasis* (18) or omits critical points in the process. I therefore find the viewpoint descriptions in Nick Rozanski and Eoin Woods' *Software Systems Architecture*[65] useful because they don't prescribe a fixed notation, but highlight concerns and pitfalls. Nick and Eoin also separate *perspectives* from *views*. When sketching an architecture you are most likely interested in a specific perspective, such as performance and security, that spans multiple viewpoints, for example a deployment or functional view.

Visuals

Each artist has his or her own style and to some degree architecture sketches will also differ. I am not a big fan of molding all system documentation into a single notation because we are not creating a system specification (that's in the code), but a sketch that gives humans a better vehicle to reason about the system. For me, it's important that every visual feature of the notation has meaning in the context, or perspective, that we are analyzing. Otherwise, it's just noise. Of course, the diagram must not only show the components but also *their relationships* (22).

The best diagrams are rich in expressiveness but don't require a legend because the notation is intuitive from the start or because the viewer can learn the notation from simple examples and apply what he or she learned to more complex aspects of the diagram. This is very much how user interfaces work: no user wants to read a long manual, but will use what they see to build a mental model and use it to set expectations for how more complex features should

[65]Rozanski, Woods: Software Systems Architecture, Addison-Wesley, 2011

work. Why not think of a diagram as a user interface? You may feel that it lacks interactivity, and you are right, but viewers *navigate* complex diagrams very much like users navigate user interfaces.

Architecture Therapy

Grady Booch drew analogies between having teams depicting their architecture and family therapy[66], which asks children to draw a picture of their family in a method referred to as Kinetic Family Drawings (KFD). The drawings give therapists insight into the family dynamics, such as proximity, hierarchy, or behavioral patterns. I have experienced the same with development teams, so you shouldn't outright discard their drawings as meaningless or incomplete, but derive insight into the team's thinking and hierarchy from them: is the database in the middle of it all? Maybe the schema designer is calling the shots in the team (I know a case of that happening). Are there many boxes, but no lines? Probably the team's thinking is focused on structural concerns but ignores system behavior. This is often the case when the architect is too far removed from code and operational aspects.

That's wrong! Do it again!

A common situation when sketching an architecture for someone else is them stating "this is wrong!" This is a good thing - it means that you discovered a mismatch between your and their under-standing. If you hadn't drawn it, you would have never realized. Also, if you assume you are a reasonable proxy for subsequent consumers of the diagram, you also saved them from the same misunderstanding. Therefore, sketching out architecture is almost always an iterative process. Bring an eraser.

---

[66]Booch: Draw Me a Picture; in IEEE Software, vol.28, no. 1, Jan/Feb 2011

21. Diagram-Driven Design

Cheating in a picture is much harder than cheating in words.

This is not an architecture.

A few years ago, the Crested Butte Enterprise Architecture Summit once again proved that sticking a bunch of geeks into a remote town and injecting alcohol into the mix can lead to impressive or at least creative results. In our case, the result was an A-Z list of 26 new development strategies, starting from ADD – Activity Driven Development and ending on ZDD- Zero Defect Development. DDD was dedicated to Eric Evan's fantastic book *Domain-driven Design*[67]. However, another "DDD" sprang to mind: *Diagram-Driven Design*.

When talking about Diagram-Driven Design, I don't mean generating code from *UML* diagrams. I am pretty firmly rooted in Martin Fowler's *UML as Sketch*[68] camp, meaning UML is a picture to aid human comprehension, not a programming language or specification. If people question my view, I simply quote Grady

---

[67]Evans: *Domain-Driven Design*, Addison-Wesley, 2003
[68]http://martinfowler.com/bliki/UmlAsSketch.html

Booch, who as co-creator of the UML remarked that "The UML was never intended to be a programming language."[69] Instead, I am talking about a picture that conveys important concepts – the proverbial big picture that does not get caught up in irrelevant details.

Presentation Skills – More than a Wide Stance

While working for Google in Japan, I created and taught a class on presentation skills for engineers, which included the usual ideas of using strong, impactful visuals inspired by books like *Presentation Zen*[70]. Following my own advice equipped me with high-resolution graphics of confident managers, fuel gauges indicating that your mileage may indeed vary, shoes that apparently do not fit all, and so on. Still, however impactful fancy graphics may be, for most technical presentations a wide stance, deep voice, and Steve Jobs-like hand gestures (turtleneck optional) are unlikely to teach the audience how your system architecture works.

Instead, you need "meat": what design alternatives did the team have? How do they differ? What design principles made you choose one over the other? What are the main building blocks of the systems and how *do they interact* (22)? How did you track down that performance bottleneck and what did you learn from it? When Garr Reynolds, the author of *Presentation Zen*, came to Google to talk about his book, he acknowledged that technical discussions often require detailed diagrams or even snippets of source code, which he suggested to provide in form of a hand-out instead of including it in visual aids. Still, most presentations I see contain bullet points, source code, or diagrams to explain technical concepts and detail.

Ed Tufte already put bullet points through the grinder by blaming them for the inaction that led to the Columbia space shuttle

---

[69]Objective View Magazine, Issue #12, http://www.ovmag.com/OV12.pdf
[70]Reynolds: *Presentation Zen: Simple Ideas on Presentation Design and Delivery*, New Riders, 2011

disaster[71] upon re-entry (and he may not be wrong judging from the slides they put together). Death by PowerPoint was immortalized by a Dilbert comic strip as early as 2000. You can't fit a lot of source code on a slide either, especially if you are using a verbose language with checked exceptions. That leaves you with diagrams as your main communication vehicle for technical concepts.

Diagramming Skills

It seems that Visio's default 10 point font size and skimpy line width coupled with poor user judgment caused almost as much damage to diagramming as PowerPoint and its endless supply of bullet points (aided by the "autosize" feature) did to textual presentations. True, the tool isn't solely responsible (guns don't kill people...), but Visio's default settings, which are tuned for detailed engineering schematics, lure the user into creating something that is unsuitable for projecting the proverbial big picture on the wall. A sequel to my presentation skills class therefore takes on technical diagrams, starting with basic advice like:

- Make sure your text is readable by using sans serif fonts of decent size and good color contrast. It's amazing how many slides contain 10pt *Times Roman* font in dark gray on dark blue background. "I know you can't read this" isn't a good introduction into a slide. It's even more shocking to see that slides with tiny fonts often consist to 50% of empty space that could have been used for larger boxes and larger fonts.
- Reduce visual noise by making sure elements are properly aligned and have consistent form and shape (e.g. border widths, arrowhead sizes etc). If things look different, make sure that it *expresses meaning* (22).
- Increase the size of arrow heads on the lines so that they can be more easily spotted. If direction isn't critical to understanding the diagram, then omit the arrowheads.

---

[71]http://www.edwardtufte.com/bboard/q-and-a-fetch-msg?msg_id=0001yB

As I went on to explain how to establish a consistent visual vocabulary, or omit unnecessary details, I recognized that many of the diagramming techniques I was describing also contribute to good system design in general. Thus, *Diagram-Driven Design* became a reality!

Diagramming as Design Technique

Once you embrace diagramming as a design technique you can apply a number of methods to aid with your system design:

Establish a Visual Vocabulary and Viewpoints

Good diagrams use a consistent visual language. A box means something (for example, a component, a class, a process), a solid line something else (maybe a build dependency, data flow, or an HTTP request), and a dashed line something else yet. No, you don't need a *Meta-Object Facility* and correctness-proven semantics, but you need to have an idea what element or relationship you are depicting how. Picking this visual vocabulary is important to define the architectural viewpoint you are going to concern yourself with, such as source code dependencies, run-time dependencies, call trees, or allocation of processes to machines.

Any diagram or description merely represents an abstract *model* of the system, as the opening paragraph of William Kent's "Data and Reality"[72] aptly reminds us: "rivers do not have dotted lines in them and freeways are not painted red." It's OK to use a bit of artistic license.

Good design is often tied to the ability to think in abstractions. Diagrams are personified abstractions and can be instrumental in this process.

---

[72]Kent: Data and Reality, Technics Publications, 3rd edition, 2012

Limit the Levels of Abstraction

One of the most frequent problems I encounter in technical documents is a wild mix of different levels of abstraction (the same problem can be found in source code). For example, the way configuration data affects a system's behavior may be described like this:

> The system configuration is stored in an XML file, whose "timetravel" entry can be set to either `true` or `false`. The file is read from the local file system or alternatively from the network but then you need NFS access or have Samba installed. It uses a SAX parser to preserve memory. The "Config" class, which reads these settings, is a singleton because...

In these few sentences we learn about the file format, project design decisions, implementation detail, performance optimizations and more. It's rather unlikely that a single reader is actually interested in this smörgåsbord of facts.

Now try to draw a picture of this paragraph! It will be nearly impossible to get all these concepts onto a single sheet of paper. Drawing a picture thus forces us to clean up our thinking by considering one level of abstraction at a time. While drawing a picture doesn't automagically make the problem of mixing abstractions disappear, it puts it in your face much more than a meandering chain of prose, which from afar may not look all that bad. A well-known German proverb proclaims that "Papier ist geduldig" (paper is patient), meaning paper is unlikely to object to what garbage you scribble on it. Diagrams are a little less patient.

Reduce to the Essence

Billboard-size database schema posters, which include every single table, stick to a single level of abstraction, but are still fairly useless because they *don't place an emphasis* (18), especially when shrunk down to fit on a single presentation slide. Omit unimportant detail to concentrate on what's relevant!

Find Balance and Harmony

Limiting the levels of abstraction and scope does not yet guarantee a useful diagram. Good diagrams lay out important entities such that they are logically grouped, relationships become naturally clear, and an overall balance and harmony emerges. If such a balance doesn't emerge, it may just be that your system doesn't have one.

I once reviewed a relatively small module of code that consisted of a rather entangled mess of classes and relationships. When the developer and I tried to document this module, we just couldn't come up with a half-decent way to sketch up what's going on. After a lot of drawing and erasing we came up with a picture that vaguely resembled a data processing pipeline. We subsequently refactored the entangled code to match this new system metaphor. It improved the structure and testability of the code significantly, thanks to diagram-driven design!

Indicate Degrees of Uncertainty

When looking at a piece of code, one can always figure out *what* was done, but it's much harder to understand *why* it was done. It can be even more difficult to understand which decisions were made consciously and which ones simply happened. When creating diagrams, we have more tools at hand to express these nuances: for example, you can use a hand-drawn sketch to convey that it is merely a basis for discussion as opposed to an engineering blueprint that represents the ultimate truth. Many books, including Eric Evans', use this technique effectively to avoid the *precision vs. accuracy dilemma*: "next week it will be roughly 15.235 degrees". Don't make precise-looking slides if you know they aren't accurate.

Diagrams are Art

Diagrams can (and should) be beautiful – little works of art, even. I am a firm believer that system design has a close relationship to art and (non-technical) design. Both visual and technical design start with a blank slate and virtually unlimited possibilities. Decisions are often influenced by multiple, usually conflicting forces. Good design resolves these forces to create a functional solution, which attains a good balance and some degree of beauty. This may explain why many of my friends who are great (software) designers and architects have an artistic vein or at least interest.

No Silver Bullet(point)

Not all diagrams are useful as a design technique. Drawing a messy picture won't make your poor design any better. Beautiful *marchitecture*[73] diagrams, which have little to do with the actual system being built, are also of limited value. In technical discussions, though, I have observed many occasions where drawing a good diagram has greatly improved the conversation and the resulting design decisions. If you are unable to draw a good diagram (and it isn't due to lack of skill), it may just be because your actual system structure is not what it should be.

---

[73]*marchitecture* denotes marketing pictures disguised as architecture

22. Drawing the Line

Architecture without lines likely isn't one.

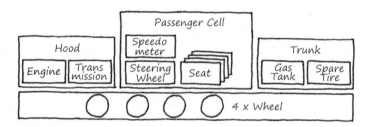

A functional architecture of a car

The picture above depicts the architecture of a car. All the important components are there, including their relationships: the engine's under the hood; passenger seats are appropriately located inside the passenger compartment, close to the steering wheel; wheels are assembled nicely at the bottom of the car in the chassis. This diagram appears to fulfill most definitions of architecture (except my favorite one because I am *looking for decisions* (9)).

However, it does precious little to help you understand how a car functions: could you omit the gas tank as it's far away from the engine, anyway? Are engine and transmission side-by-side under the hood by coincidence or do they have a special relationship? Does the car need exactly 4 wheels or will 3 also do? If you had to build the car in stages, what subset would make sense to assemble first? Would just the cabin with the seats be a good start? How can you tell a good car from a bad one? Which aspects are common in virtually all cars (e.g. the wheels being at the bottom) and which ones vary (Porsche 911, VW Beetle or DeLorean owners would be quick to point out that their engine isn't under the hood)?

The picture doesn't really answer any of these questions. It depicts the location of the components but it doesn't convey their relationships or function in the overall system "car". While the picture is factually correct and actually reasonably detailed, it doesn't allow us to reason much about the system it is describing, especially its behavior. Coincidentally, it may also not be a good example of *Diagram-driven Design* (21).

Behold the Line!

The critical element that's missing in the picture are lines connecting the components. Without lines, it's quite difficult to represent rich relationships. The line is so important that boxes, labels, and lines suffice to make up Kent Beck's only half-joking Galactic Modeling Language[74]. Without lines, there wouldn't be much of a modeling language left. Also, as often stated, "the lines are more interesting than the boxes." Where does stuff usually go wrong? In the integration between two well-tested pieces. Where do I need to look to achieve strong or loose coupling? Between the boxes. How do I tell a well-structured architecture from a *Big Ball of Mud*[75]? By the lines.

Therefore, if I see an architecture diagram without any connecting lines, I am skeptical as to whether it qualifies as a meaningful depiction of an architecture. Unfortunately, many diagrams I see fail this basic test.

The Metamodel

Stating that the picture at the beginning doesn't show any relationships isn't quite true. The picture does contain two primary relationships between components:

---

[74]http://c2.com/cgi/wiki?GalacticModelingLanguage
[75]Foote, Harrison, Rohnert: Pattern Languages of Program Design 4, Addison Wesley, 1999

- *Containment,* i.e. one box is enclosed by another.
- *Proximity,* i.e. some boxes are close to each other while others are further apart.

Containment corresponds to real-world semantics in this drawing: seats are actually *contained* inside the passenger cell, and the hood (the engine compartment to be more precise) houses engine and transmission. Engine and transmission are also next to each other, giving them *proximity,* which underlines them sharing a strong relationship: one makes little sense without the other. But the *proximity* semantics in this picture are relatively weak: the gas tank and spare tire are also next to each other, but for the function of the car this doesn't have any meaning. The vague correspondence of proximity in the diagram to real-life proximity has no relationship to function and thus renders an odd mix of a logical and physical representation.

I routinely challenge diagrams that limit relationships between components to containment. Such diagrams make it difficult to reason about the system, as seen in the car example above. Reasoning about the system is one of the main purposes of drawing an (architecture) diagram, so we need to do better.

Diagrams that are only based on containment and proximity generally could have been just as easily represented as an indented bullet list: sub-bullets are contained by outer bullets and bullets next to each other are in proximity. In our example, you would end up with a list like this (showing only a portion to avoid *death by bullet points*):

- Hood
    - Engine
    - Transmission
- Passenger Cell
    - Speedometer

– Steering Wheel
– 4 seats

In this case, the picture doesn't say the proverbial 1000 words. The list and the picture are just different *projections* of the same tree structure. And people say intentional programming[76] is difficult! You may like the picture better than the list, but you must be aware that both representations have the same richness, or poorness, of expression. The picture adds the size and shape of the boxes, which aren't represented in the textual list, but the semantics of size and shape in our example are unclear: all components are rectangles, but the wheels are circles. It's a crude approximation of reality, but for reasoning about the system it doesn't add much.

The Semantics of Semantics

When I was told for the first time that "UML sequence diagrams have weak semantics", I was doubtful whether this rather academic statement had any relevance for me as a normal programmer. The short answer is: "yes, it does." Prior to UML 2, sequence diagrams depicted only one possible sequence of interactions between objects, albeit allowing for concurrency. They couldn't express the complete set of legal interaction sequences, such as loops (repeating interactions) or branches (either-or choices). Because loops and branches are some of the most fundamental control flow constructs, sequence diagrams' weak semantics rendered them essentially useless as a specification. UML 2 improved the semantics but at the cost of much reduced readability.

Why worry so much about the semantics of a diagram? The purpose of design diagrams or engineering drawings is to give viewers an understanding of the system, particularly the system behavior. A drawing is a model, so it's by definition wrong (see *Making Decisions* (6)). However, it can be useful, e.g. by allowing the viewer

---

[76]http://c2.com/cgi/wiki?IntentionalProgramming

to reason about the system. The visual elements, such as boxes and lines, must neatly map to concepts in the abstract model so the viewer can build the model in his or her head. For the viewer to grasp the *meaning* of the drawing, the visual elements need semantics: semantics is the study of meaning.

Elements - Relationship - Behavior

Without lines, it's impossible to ascertain a system's behavior. It's like listing the ingredients for a meal without the recipe. Whether something tasty comes out primarily depends on the way it's prepared: potatoes can turn into French fries, gratin, boiled potatoes, mashed potatoes, baked potatoes, fried potatoes, hash browns, and more. A meaningful architecture diagram, therefore, needs to depict the relationships between components and provide semantics for these relationships.

Electric circuit diagrams provide a canonical example of system behavior that depends heavily on connections between components. One of the most versatile elements in analog circuitry is the operational amplifier, short *op-amp*. Paired with a few resistors and a capacitor or two, this element can act as a comparator, amplifier, inverted amplifier, differentiator, filter, oscillator, wave generator, and much more – op-amp circuits fill many books. The system's behavior, which varies widely, doesn't depend on the list of elements, but solely on how they are connected. In the world of IT, a database can act as a cache, ledger, file storage, data store, content store, queue, configuration input, and much more. How the database is connected to its surrounding elements is fundamental, just like the op-amp.

Architecture Diagrams

If you feel that this is about as much as one could and should say about a contrived sketch of a car, rest assured that I get to see many architecture diagrams without any lines. These diagrams do depict proximity, simply because some boxes have to be next to each other, but whether any semantics are tied to this fact remains unclear. If you are lucky, proximity represents a form of "layering" from top to bottom, which in turn implies a dependency from things on "top" to things "further down". In the worst case, proximity was defined by the order in which the author drew the boxes.

So-called "capability diagrams" or "functional architectures" are particularly likely to be devoid of lines. These diagrams tend to list (pun intended) capabilities that are needed to perform a certain business function. For example, to manage customer relationships you need customer channels, campaign management, a reporting dashboard, etc. The set of capabilities forms a "laundry list" of things that are needed, but aren't closer to architecture than listing windows, doors, roof for a house. I, therefore, prefer such input to be represented as textual lists so that this distinction becomes clear. Wrapping text in boxes doesn't constitute architecture.

UML

Speaking of lines, UML has a beautiful abundance of line styles: in a class diagram, *classes* (boxes) can be connected through association (a simple line), aggregation (with a hollow diamond on one end), composition (a solid diamond), or generalization (triangle). Navigability can be indicated by an open arrow and a dependency by a dashed line. On top of this, *multiplicities*, e.g. a truck having four to eight wheels but only one engine, can be added to the relationship lines. In fact, UML class diagrams allow so many kinds of relationships that Martin Fowler decided to split the discussion into two separate chapters inside his defining book *UML Distilled*[77]. Interestingly, UML allows *composition* to be visually expressed through a line or as *containment*, i.e. drawing one box inside the other.

---

[77]Fowler: UML Distilled: A Brief Guide to the Standard Object Modeling Language (3rd Edition), Addison-Wesley Professional, 2003

With such a rich visual vocabulary, why invent your own? The challenge with UML notation is that you can appreciate the nuances of the relationship semantics between classes only if you have in fact read *UML Distilled* or the UML specification. That's why such diagrams aren't as useful when addressing a broad audience: the visual translation of solid diamond vs. hollow diamond or solid line vs. dotted line isn't immediately intuitive. This is where containment works well: a box inside another is easily understood without having to add a legend.

Beware of Extremes

As so often, the opposite of bad is also troublesome. I have seen diagrams where elements have different shapes, sizes, colors, and border widths; connecting lines have solid arrows, open arrows, no arrows, are dotted, dashed, and of different color. These cases either result from sloppiness, in which case the visual variation has no meaning and is simply "noise", or from a metamodel that's so rich (or convoluted) that a diagram likely isn't the right way to convey it. The rule I apply is that any visual variation in a diagram should have meaning, i.e. semantics. If it doesn't, the variance should be eliminated to reduce visual noise, which only distracts the viewer and, worse yet, may cause the viewer to interpret this noise as semantics that were in fact never intended. As you cannot look inside the viewer's head, such misunderstandings or misinterpretations are difficult to detect. In short: making all boxes the same size won't crimp your artistic talent but will make clear to the viewer that the model behind the diagram considers all boxes to have the same properties.

The standard text on charting and diagramming is Tufte's *The Visual Display of Quantitative Information*[78] plus his subsequent books. While the books initially focus on display of numeric information, later volumes cover broader aspects, including many

---

[78]Tufte: The Visual Display of Quantitative Information, Graphics Pr, 2001

examples that package complex concepts into diagrams that remain crisp and easy to grasp.

Elements of Style

Most architects will develop their own visual style over time. My diagrams tend to be bold with large lettering because I value readability over subtle aesthetics. As a result, my diagrams look like cartoons to some viewers, but I am fine with that. My diagrams virtually always have lines, but I keep the lines' semantics to two or at most three concepts. Each type of relationship that I depict with lines should be intuitive. For example, I may depict a data flow with broad, gray arrows, while control flow is shown in thin, black lines. The line width suggests that a large amount of data flows through the system's data flow while the control flow is much smaller, but significant. The best visual style, borrowed from advice on writing, is the one "that keeps solely in view the thought one wants to convey"[79].

---

[79]Barzun, Jacques: Simple & Direct, Harper Perennial, 2001

Organizations

Architects in the enterprise live right at the intersection of the technical and business worlds. Thus, they interact with a variety of players from various levels and functions in the organization: CIOs and COOs, business operations heads, sales staff, IT operations, developers, etc. Therefore, a good architect needs to not only understand the interplay between system components, but also the interplay between individuals and departments in a large and dynamic system called *organization*.

The Static View

The most common depiction of an organization is the organizational chart ("org chart"). These charts depict who reports to whom and one can measure their importance by how far they are from the CEO. In my case, I am at level 1 in my division and level 3 globally, assuming you count from 0 in good computer science tradition: CEO - Group COO - Divisional CEO - myself. For a large organization, this is not bad at all – many people are at level 6 or 7. Computer-science educated folks may recognize an org chart as a tree, a non-cyclical, connected directed graph with a single *root* (math folks consider trees to be undirected, but that's fine also).

The Dynamic View

Static structures tell us little about how people interact to make the business work, though. The engineering, manufacturing, marketing, and finance departments may be depicted as separate pillars of the organizational pyramid. However, in reality engineering has to design a product that can be easily and reliably manufactured, marketed to customers, and sold at a profit. How well organizations work is rarely defined by the organization's structure - most organizations will have the aforementioned functions - but by how they interact: how slow or fast are their development cycles, do they work in a waterfall or an agile model, who talks to customers (who interestingly are not depicted in the org chart) ?

Coworkers also routinely talk to each other to solve problems without following the lines in the organizational pyramid. This is a good thing because otherwise managers would quickly become communication bottlenecks. In many cases the org chart depicts the *control flow* of the organization, e.g. to give budget approvals, while the *data flow* is much more open and dynamic. Ironically, the way people actually work with each other is rarely depicted in a diagram. Part of the reason may be that this data is difficult to gather, the other part may be that it doesn't look nearly as neat as the org chart pyramid.

As people coordinate and communicate via systems, the actual, dynamic organizational structure can be more easily observed. For example, if developers collaborate via a version control system, one can analyze code reviews or check-in approvals to see the real collaboration taking place. Google had another interesting system that allowed you to see which persons are sitting nearby a given person. As interaction and collaboration are often still based on ad-hoc conversations, physical proximity can be a better predictor of collaboration patterns than the org chart structure.

The Matrix (Not the Movie)

In large organizations, people may have multiple reporting lines: a "dotted-line" to their project or program manager and a "solid line" to their department or "line manager". Such an arrangement is often part of a so-called *matrix organization* where people report horizontally to the project and vertically to their manager. Or is it the other way around? If you are not sure and find this a little confusing, you are not alone. High-performance delivery organizations generally shun such arrangements, making sure people are fully assigned to, and responsible for, a single project. I often jest that I want all people working on a project to be on the same boat without life vests and no rescue lines to other parts of the organization. A team needs a shared success or, if it so happens, shared failure. Don't worry, they are all able to swim.

Organizations as Systems

As architects we know well how to design systems: when to apply horizontal scaling, loose coupling, caching etc. We often are also trained in systems thinking, which teaches us how to reason about the relationship between elements in a system and the overall system behavior, driven for example by positive or negative feedback loops. However, we often hesitate to apply such rational thinking to organizations because organizations have a very human face, which makes us feel bad if we degrade our nice and not-so-nice coworkers into *Boxes-and-lines* (22) of some system architecture. However, large organizations behave much more like systems than like individuals. Therefore, as architects we should apply our rational systems thinking to understanding and influencing large organizations.

Organizations as People

All rational reasoning aside, organizations are made up of individuals. We must also not forget that for many of them work is just a small part of their lives: they have families to take care of, bills to pay, doctors to visit, home repairs to make, or hangovers from the party last night to overcome. Understanding organizations depends on understanding people's emotions and motivations. This can be a stretch for left-brain-type architects, but one they need to make. Consider this yoga for your brain.

Navigating Large Organizations

This chapter presents different angles of understanding organizations:

- How command-and-control structures are intended to work and why they don't work that way because *Control is an Illusion* (23)
- The reasons why *Pyramids* (24) went out of vogue 4500 years ago, but are still widely used in IT systems and organizational charts.
- How *Black Markets* (25) compensate for the inflexibility of command-and-control, but cause a new set of problems.
- How experience in scaling distributed computer systems can be applied to *Scaling an Organization* (26)
- Why fast-moving things can appear chaotic while slow-moving things seem well coordinated when in reality it's often the opposite due to *Slow-motion Chaos* (27).
- Why governance by decree is difficult and better done by *Planting Ideas through Inception* (28).

23. Control is an Illusion

It's when you're told exactly what you want to hear.

Who's in control here?

While working in Asia I became accustomed to sharing a bit of personal detail before presenting to a group of people. I liked the idea because it didn't have the flavor of bragging about professional accomplishments, but rather to give the audience an impression about your background to better understand what shaped your thinking. In a presentation to a group of CEEMA (Central-Eastern Europe, Middle-East and Africa region) COOs and CIOs, I once opened with a slide summarizing my core beliefs in the form of *pin buttons* that many people used to wear in the 1980s. The one slogan that received immediate attention was "Control is an Illusion". Even more attention drew my explanation that you just feel that you have control when people tell you what you want to hear.

The Illusion

How can control be an illusion? "Having control" is based on the assumption that a direction set from top-down is actually being followed and has the desired effect. And this can be a big illusion. How would you know that it does, if you are simply sitting at the top, pushing (control) buttons instead of working alongside the staff? You may rely on management status reports, but then you make another major assumption that the presented information reflects reality. This may be yet another big illusion.

Steven Denning uses the term "semblance of control" in contrast to "actual control" for this phenomenon in large organizations. A more cynical version would be to claim that the inmates are running the asylum. In either case, not the state you want your organization to be in.

Control Circuits

To understand where the discrepancy between perceived reality and real reality originates, it helps to have a brief look at control theory. Control circuits, such as a room thermostat, illustrate that control isn't a one-way street: turning the furnace on and off may seem like controlling a part of the system, but an actual control circuit keeps the room temperature constant based on a closed feedback loop: turning the furnace on heats the room; the thermostat measures the room temperature and turns the furnace off when the desired temperature is reached. The control circuit is based on one or more *sensors*, such as the room temperature sensor, and one or more *actors*, such as the furnace, which influence the system.

The feedback loop compensates for external factors such as the outside temperature or someone opening the window. The control loop doesn't determine up-front how warm the room should be by running the heater for a pre-computed amount of time. Instead, the control circuit is set to a specific target and the "controller" uses sensors to measure continuously whether the target is achieved and acts accordingly. One can quickly draw the analogy to project planning that commonly attempts to predict all factors up-front and subsequently tries to eliminate all disturbances. It's like running the heater for exactly 2 hours and then blaming the cold weather for the room not being warm enough.

Smart Control

Some control circuits take in more feedback signals and refine how they drive the system. For example, my heater measures the outside temperature to predict energy loss through windows and walls. Google's "Nest" thermostat takes it a step further: it takes in additional information, such as the weather forecast (the sun helps warm the house), and when you are usually home or away. It also learns about the system behavior, such as the inertia of the heating system (turning the furnace off just as the room reaches the target temperature is likely to overheat the house as there's heat capacity left in the radiators) or how well insulated the house is (which impacts how much more heat is needed when it's cold outside), "Nest" is called a "learning" or "smart" thermostat – it takes in more feedback and optimizes what it does based on that feedback. It would be nice if we consistently applied the same terminology to project managers.

A Two-way street

Jeff Sussna describes the importance of feedback loops in his book *Designing Delivery*[80], drawing on the notion of *cybernetics*. While most people think of cyborgs and terminators when they hear the

---

[80]Jeff Sussna: Designing Delivery, O'Reilly, 2015

term, cybernetics is actually a field of study that deals with "control and communication in the animal and the machine". Such control and communication is almost always based on a closed signaling loop.

When we portray large organizations as "command-and-control" structures, we often focus only on the top-down steering part, and less on the feedback from the "sensors". But not using the sensors means one is flying blind, possibly with a feeling of control, but one that's disconnected from reality. It's like driving a car and turning the steering wheel when you have no lights and have no clue where the car is actually headed – a very dumb idea. It's shocking to see how such behavior bordering on absurdity can establish itself in large organizations or systems.

Problems on the way up

Even if an organization uses sensors, e.g. by obtaining the infamous status reports, not all is necessarily well. Anyone who has heard the term *Watermelon status* understands: these are the projects whose status is "green" on the outside, but "red" on the inside, meaning they are presented as going well, but in reality suffer from serious issues. Corporate project managers and status reporters aren't straight-out liars, but they do tend to take some literary license to make their project look good or are just overly optimistic. "700 happy passengers reach New York after Titanic's maiden voyage" is also factually correct, but not the status report you may want to get.

Observing how much trust some senior executives place in Power-Point slides might make you believe that it not only has a built-in spell checker but also a lie detector. Digital companies are generally suspicious of fabricated presentations and "massaged" messages, but instead believe in hard data, preferably rendered in live metrics dashboards.

Google's Mobile Ads team in Japan reviewed the performance of all ads experiments, run as A/B tests, every week and decided which experiments should be accepted into production, which ones should be rejected, and which ones needed to run longer in order to become conclusive. The decisions were based on hard user data, not projections or promises.

At times this can be frustrating because getting a solution running doesn't yet earn you much praise – that's expected anyway. Praise comes once you have attention and traffic from actual users – data that's much harder to fabricate.

Saupreiß, net so Damischer

When people speak about command-and-control structures, they are quick to cite the military, which, after all, is run by "commanders". The military organization most equated with stodginess and "iron discipline" is the Prussian army. For people living in Bavaria in the south of Germany, Prussia is eternalized in the concept of the "Saupreiß", the *Prussian Pig*, a derogatory term referring to people born in or north of Frankfurt, like myself.

Ironically, the Prussian military understood very well that one-way control is an illusion. Carl von Clausewitz wrote a 1000-page tome *On War* in the early 1800s, in which he cites sources of *friction*: the external gap between desired and actual outcomes (uncertainty) and the internal gap between plans and the actions of an organization. Stephen Bungay extends this concept in his book *The Art of Action*[81] into three gaps: the *knowledge gap* between what you'd like to know and actually do know, the *alignment gap* between plans and actions, and the *effects gap* between what you expect your actions to achieve and what actually happens. The Prussians knew that trying to eliminate these gaps won't work.

---

[81]Bungay: The Art of Action, Nicholas Brealey Publishing, 2010

Instead, the concept of *Auftragstaktik* replaced a concrete order with a *mission* or *directive*, which allows the troops to adjust to unforeseen circumstances without having to report back to central command. Auftragstaktik doesn't mean people are left to do whatever they deem appropriate. It's based on discipline, but *active discipline*, one that respects the commander's intentions, as opposed to *passive obedience*, which demands blind execution. So the "Preißn" weren't so stodgy after all.

Actual Control

Translating from the military context back into the world of large-scale IT organizations, how do you obtain actual control, not illusionary control, in an organization? In my experience you need three elements:

1. *Enablement*: It may sound trivial, but first you need to enable people to perform their work. Sadly, corporate IT knows many mechanisms that *disable* people: HR processes that restrict recruiting, servers that take 4 weeks to be provisioned, *black markets* (25) that are not accessible to new hires. A thermostat connected to a furnace with a plugged gas line won't do much good.
2. *Autonomy*: Let people figure out how to achieve their goals because they have the shortest *feedback cycles* (32) that allow them to learn and improve. You let the thermostat decide when to turn the furnace on and off, so do the same for your teams!
3. *Pressure*: Set very specific goals that the team needs to achieve, e.g. revenue generated or quantifiable user engagement. A thermostat is only useful if someone sets the desired temperature.

This system won't work if you omit one or more elements: pressure without enablement will lead to zero progress, but lots of frustration. Autonomy without pressure will have teams just playing around. And pressure without autonomy will stifle innovation.

Early Warning System

While a control circuit's job is to keep a system in a steady state without someone having to monitor it, observing its behavior can be useful in a larger context. For example, if the air filter in a forced-air heating system becomes clogged or the furnace collects soot, it will take longer to warm the house under otherwise identical conditions of room and outside temperature. A smart control system that measures the length of the thermostat duty cycle can give a hint that the system is no longer operating as efficiently as it used to. The "smart" Nest thermostat includes such a function. Therefore, a control loop shouldn't be a "black box", but should expose health metrics based on what it has "learned".

This is one reason I am cautious with much-touted cloud features like server auto-scaling, which are able to absorb sudden load spikes without human intervention, but can also mask serious problems. For example, if a new version of the software performs poorly, the infrastructure may attempt to auto-compensate this problem by deploying more servers.

If you consider control as a means of steering towards a target while compensating for external influences, plus carefully observing system behavior, then it's in fact not an illusion.

24. They don't build'em quite like that anymore

IT's love of pyramids

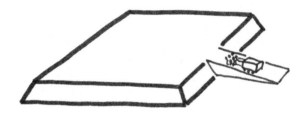

The Great Pyramid at 30% completion. Effort completion, that is.

The great pyramids are impressive buildings and attract hordes of tourists even several millennia after their construction. The attraction results not only from the engineering marvel, such as the perfect alignment and balance, but also from the fact that pyramids are quite rare. Besides the US One Dollar Bill, you'll only find them in Egypt, central America, and IT organizations!

Why IT Architects Love Pyramids

Pyramids are a fairly common sight in IT architecture diagrams and tend to give architects, especially the ones nearer to the penthouse, a noticeable sense of satisfaction. In most cases, the pyramid diagram indicates a layering concept with a base layer that includes functionality commonly needed by the upper layers. For example, the base layer could contain an open-source application framework, the middle layer a custom application, and the tip customer-specific *Configuration* (11). Layering is a very popular and useful concept in systems architecture because it constrains dependencies between system components to flow in a single direction, as opposed to a *Big Ball of Mud* (9).

Depicting the layers in the shape of a pyramid suggests that the upper layers are much smaller and more specialized than the base layers, which provide most of the common functionality. IT is enamored with this model because it implies that a large portion of the base layer code can be shared or acquired as it's identical across many businesses and applications. For example, a better object-relational mapping framework or a common business component, such as billing, are unlikely to present a competitive advantage and should simply be bought or reused. Meanwhile, necessary and valuable customizations can be performed in the "tip" with relatively little effort or by lesser skilled labor. The analogy is consistent with the pyramids of Giza, where the top 1/3 of the pyramid's height only makes up roughly 4% of the material.

Organizational Pyramids

The other place littered with pyramids are slide decks depicting organizational structures, where they refer to hierarchical structures. Almost all organizations are hierarchical: multiple people from a lower *tier* report to a single person on the next upper tier, resulting in a directed *tree* graph, which, when the root is placed on the top, resembles a pyramid. Even "flat" organizations tend to have some hierarchy as a single person generally acts as a chairman or CEO. Such a setup makes sense because directing work takes less effort than actually conducting the work, meaning an organization needs fewer managers or supervisors than workers (unless they are *Trying to buy love* (34)). Having fewer leaders also helps with consistent decision making and setting a single strategic direction.

No Pyramid Without Pharaoh

Still, there's a good reason that the idea of building pyramids was abandoned some 4500 years ago: the base layers of a pyramid require an enormous amount of material. It's estimated that the Great Pyramid of Giza consists of over 2 million blocks weighing in at several tons each. Assuming workers toiled day and night over the course of one decade, they would have had to lay an average 3 large limestone blocks per *minute*. Three quarters of the material had to be laid for the first 50m of height alone. While the result is undoubtedly impressive and long-lasting, it can hardly be called efficient. The economics of building pyramids can only function if there's an abundance of cheap or forced labor (the historians still debate whether the pyramids were built by slaves or paid workers) or a Pharaoh's unbelievable accumulation of wealth. In addition to resources, one also needs to bring a lot of patience. Building pyramids doesn't mix well with *Economies of Speed* (31). Some of the pyramids in Egypt weren't even finished during the Pharaoh's lifetime.

Functional pyramids as we find them in IT system designs face another challenge: the folks building the base layer not only have to move humongous amounts of material, they also have to anticipate the needs of the teams building the upper layers. Building a pyramid from the bottom up negates the principle of "use before reuse": designing functions to be reused later without first actually using them can be a guessing game at best. It also dangerously ignores the *Build-Measure-Learn Cycle* (32) of learning what's needed from observing actual usage.

Not limited to pyramids, but applicable to any layered system is the challenge of defining the appropriate *seams* between the layers. Done well, these seams form abstractions that hide the complexity of the layer below while leaving the layer above with *sufficient flexibility* (11). Well-working examples like abstracting packet-based network routing behind data streams (*sockets*) are rare and when implemented well, enable major transformations like the Internet.

Building Pyramids

If one is determined to build a system as a layered pyramid, then the best way to build it is from the top down: start with a specific application that delivers customer value. Once more than one application can utilize a specific feature or functionality, let the related components sift down into the lower layer of the pyramid. Doing so ensures that the base layer contains functionality that's actually needed as opposed to functions that some people, often the *Enterprise Architects* (4) far away from actual software development, believe might be needed somewhere sometime.

Anticipating some needs ahead of time, such as the much-mentioned object-relational-mapping framework, is fine. However, developers should balance the value added by the framework with the cognitive load it brings: if learning the new framework takes 3 weeks and is fraught with mistakes and frustration, it may be better to defer the framework introduction and build applications from ground up.

Building the pyramid from top-down also typically results in much more usable APIs (programming interfaces) into the lower layers because the usability of these interfaces is tested immediately. Canonical counterexamples I have seen included a service layer that forced the client to make multiple remote calls to execute a simple function. This approach was chosen by the base layer architects because it ostensibly provides more flexibility. The first client developer coding against this interface described his experience in quite unkind words mostly related to *refuse*, referring to such well-known issues as sequencing, partial failure, maintaining state, etc. The base-layer team's retort was a new *dispatcher* layer on top of their service layer to "enhance the interaction." They were building the pyramid from the bottom up.

Building pyramids is popular in IT because the completion of the pyramid's base layer provides a *proxy metric* for actual product success. It's analogous to developers' love of building frameworks: one gets to devise his or her own requirements and upon delivery of those requirements, one declares success without any actual user having validated the need nor the implementation. In other words, designing pyramid base layers allows *Penthouse Architects* (2) to purport the notion that they are connected to the engine room without facing the scrutiny of actual product development teams or, worse yet, real customers. What's ironic is that the folks highest up in the organizational pyramid love to design the bottom layers of the IT system pyramid. The reason is clear: building successful applications is harder than generic and unvalidated base layers. Unfortunately, by the time the bluff becomes apparent, the penthouse architects are almost guaranteed to have moved to another project.

Living in Pyramids

While IT building pyramids can be debated, organizational pyramids are largely a given: we all report to a boss, who reports to someone else, and so on. In large organizations, we often define our standing by how many people are "above" us in the corporate hierarchy. The key consideration for an organization is whether they actually *live* the pyramid, i.e. whether the lines of communication and decision making follow the lines in the hierarchy. If that's the case, then the organization will face severe difficulties in times that favor *Economies of Speed* (31) because pyramid structures can be efficient, but they are neither fast nor flexible: decisions travel up and down the hierarchy, often suffering from a bottleneck in the *coordination layer* (26).

Luckily, many organizations don't actually work in the patterns described by the organization chart but follow a concept of *feature teams* or *tribes*, which have complete ownership of an individual product or service: decisions are pushed down to the level of the people actually most familiar with the problem. This speeds up decision making and provides shorter feedback loops.

Some organizations are looking to speed things up by overlaying *communities of practice* over their structural hierarchy, bringing people with a common interest or area of expertise together. Communities can be useful change agents, but only if they are *empowered and have clear goals* (23). Otherwise, they run the risk of becoming *communities of leisure*, a hiding place for people to debate and socialize without measurable results.

One should wonder then why organizations are so enamored with org charts that they adorn the second slide of almost any corporate project presentation. My hypothesis is that static structures carry a lower semantic load than dynamic structures: when presented with a picture showing two boxes *A* and *B* connected by a line, the viewer can easily derive the model: *A* and *B* have a relationship. One can almost imagine two physical cardboard boxes connected by a string wire. Dynamic models are more difficult to internalize: if *A* and *B* have multiple lines between them that depict inter-action over time, possibly including conditions, parallelism, and repetition, it's much more difficult to imagine the reality the model is trying to depict. Often only an animation can make it more intuitive. Hence we are more content with static structures even though understanding a *system's behavior* (10) is generally much more useful than seeing its structure.

It Always Can Get Worse

Running an organization as a pyramid can be slow and limit feedback cycles, which are needed to drive innovation. However, some organizations have a pyramid model that's even worse: the inverse pyramid. In this model, a majority of people manage and supervise a minority of people doing actual work. Besides the apparent imbalance, the inevitable need of the *managers* to obtain updates and status reports from the *workers* is guaranteed to grind progress to a halt. Such pathetic setups can occur in organizations that used to completely *depend on external providers* (34) for IT implementation work, and are now starting to bring IT talent back in-house. It can also happen during a crisis, e.g. a major system outage, which gets so much management attention that the team spends more time preparing status calls than resolving the issue.

A second anti-pattern occurs when organizations realize the issues inherent in their hierarchical pyramid setup. They therefore supplement the existing top-down reporting organization (often referred to as *line organization*), with a new *project organization*. The combination is typically called a *matrix organization* (for once, this isn't a movie reference) as people have a horizontal reporting line into their project and a vertical reporting line into the hierarchy. However, organizations that are not yet flexible and confident enough to give project teams the necessary autonomy are prone to creating a second pyramid, the project pyramid. Now employees struggle not only with one but with two pyramids.

Building Modern Structures

If pyramids aren't the way to go, how should you build systems then? I view both systems and organizational design as an iterative, dynamic process that's driven by the need to deliver business value. When building IT systems, you should only add new components if they provide measurable value. Once you observe a sizable set of common functions, it's good to push those down into a common base layer. If you don't find such components, that's also OK. It simply means that a pyramid model doesn't fit your situation.

25. Black Markets Are Not Efficient

How things get done in a top-down organization

I got anythin' you need, bro.

A common complaint about large organizations is that they are slow and mired in processes that are designed to *exert control* (23) as opposed to supporting people in getting their work done quickly. For example, I am allowed to make technical decisions impacting tens of millions of Dollars, but must obtain management approval in order to purchase a $200 plane ticket. By the time I get the approval, often the fare has increased.

Most organizations consider such processes as crucial to keeping the organization running smoothly. "What would happen if everyone does what he or she wants?" is the common justification. Most organizations never dare to find out, not because they fear chaos and mayhem, but because they fear that everything will be fine, and the people creating and administering the processes will no longer be needed.

Black Markets to the Rescue

Ironically, under the covers of law-and-order, such organizations are intrinsically aware that their processes hinder progress. That's why these organizations tolerate a "black market" where things get done quickly and informally without following the self-imposed rules. Such black markets often take the innocuous form of needing to "know who to talk to" to get something done quickly. You need a server urgently? Instead of following the standard process, you call your buddy who can "pull a few strings." Setting up an official "priority order" process, usually for a higher price, is fine. Bypassing the process to get special favors for those who are well connected is a "black market".

Another type of black market can originate from "high up." While it's not uncommon to offer different service levels, including "VIP support", providing senior executives with support that ignores those very process or security-related constraints that were imposed by the executives in the first place, is a black market. Such a black market appears for example in the form of executives sporting sexy mobile devices that are deemed too insecure for employees, notwithstanding the fact that executive's devices often contain the most sensitive data.

Black Markets Are Rarely Efficient

These examples have in common that they are based on unwritten rules and undocumented, or sometimes secret, relationships. That's why black markets are rarely efficient, as you can see from countries where black markets constitute a major portion of the economy: black markets are difficult to control and deprive the government of much-needed tax income. They also tend to circumvent balanced allocation of resources: those with access to the black market will be able to obtain goods or favors that others cannot. Black markets therefore stifle economic development as they don't provide broad and equal access to resources. This is true for countries as much as large enterprises.

In organizations, black markets often contribute to *Slow Chaos* (27) where on the outside the organization appears to be disciplined and structured, but the reality is completely different. They also make it difficult for new members of the organization to gain traction because they lack the connections into the black market, presenting one way *Systems resist change* (10).

Black markets also cause inefficiency by forcing employees to learn the black market system. Knowing how to work the black market is undocumented organizational knowledge that's unique to the organization. The time it takes employees to learn the black market doesn't benefit the organization and presents a real, but rarely measured cost. Once acquired, the knowledge doesn't benefit the employee either, because it has no market value outside of the organization. Ironically, this effect may contribute to large organizations tolerating black markets: it aids employee retention because much of their knowledge consists of undocumented processes, special vocabulary, and black market structures, which ties them to the organization.

Worse yet, black markets break necessary feedback cycles: If procuring a server is too slow to compete in the digital world, the organization must resolve the issue and speed up that process. Circumventing it in a black market fashion gives management a false sense of security, which often goes along with fabricated heroism: "I knew we can get it done in 2 days". Amazon can get it done in a few minutes for a hundred thousand customers. The digital transformation is driven by *democratization*, i.e. giving everyone rapid access to resources. That's exactly the opposite of what a black market does.

You Cannot Outsource a Black Market

Another very costly limitation of black markets is that they cannot be outsourced. Large organizations tend to outsource commodity processes like human resources or IT operations because specialized providers have better economies of scale and lower cost structures. Naturally, outsourcing provides only the officially established, inefficient processes. Because services are now performed by a third-party provider, and processes are contractually defined, the unofficial black market bypass no longer works. Essentially, the business has subjected itself to a *work-to-rule* slowdown. Organizations that rely on an internal black market, therefore, will experience a huge loss in productivity when they outsource part of their service portfolio.

Beating the Black Market

How do you avoid running the organization via a black market? More control and governance could be one approach: just like the DEA cracks down on the black market for drugs, you could identify and shut down the black market traders. However, one must recall that the IT organization's black market isn't engaged in trading illegal substances. Rather, people circumvent processes that don't allow them to get their work done. Knowing that overambitious control processes caused the black market in the first place makes more control and governance an unlikely solution. Still, some organizations will be tempted to do so, which is a perfect example of doing exactly the opposite of what has the desired effect (see *Every System is Perfect* (10)).

The only way to avoid a black market is to build an efficient "white" market, one that doesn't hinder progress, but enables it. An efficient white market reduces people's desire to build an alternate black market system, which does take some effort after all. Trying to shut down the black market without offering a functioning white market is likely to result in resistance and substantial reduction in productivity. Self-service systems are a great tool to starve black markets because they remove the human connection and friction by giving everyone equal access, thus democratizing the process. If you can order IT infrastructure through a self-explanatory tool that provides fast provisioning times, there's much less motivation to do it "through the back door". Automating undocumented processes is cumbersome, though, and often unwelcome because it may highlight the *Slow Chaos* (27).

Feedback and Transparency

Black markets generally originate as a response to cumbersome processes, which result from process designers taking the reporting or control point-of-view: inserting a checkpoint or *quality gate* at every step provides accurate progress tracking and valuable metrics. However, it makes people using the process jump through an endless sequence of hurdles to get anything done. That's the reason I have never seen a single user-friendly HR or expense reporting system. Forcing people designing processes to use them for their own daily work can highlight the amount of friction the processes create. This means no more VIP support, but support that's good enough for everyone to use. HR teams should apply for their own job openings to see how painful the process is (I applied to my own job openings for that very reason).

Transparency is a good antidote to black markets. Black markets are inherently non-transparent, providing benefit only only to a small subset of people. Once users gain full transparency of the official processes, such as ordering a server, they may be less inclined to want to order one from the black market, which does carry some overhead and uncertainty. Therefore, full transparency should be embedded into an organization's systems as a main principle.

Replacing a black market with an efficient, democratic white market also makes *control less of an illusion* (23): if users use official, documented, and automated processes, the organization can observe actual behavior and exert governance, e.g. by requiring approvals or issuing usage quotas. No such mechanisms exist for black markets.

The main hurdle to drying up black markets is that improving processes has a measurable up-front cost while the cost of the black market is usually not measured. This gap leads to the *cost of no change* (29) being perceived as being low, which in turn reduces the incentive to change.

26. Scaling an Organization

How to Scale an Organization? The same way you scale a system!

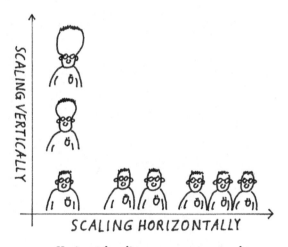

Horizontal scaling seems more natural

The digital world is all about scalability: millions of websites, billions of hits per month, petabytes of data, more tweets, more images uploaded. To make this work, architects have learned a ton about scaling systems: make services stateless and horizontally scalable, minimize synchronization points to maximize throughput, keep transaction scope local, avoid synchronous remote communication, use clever caching strategies, and shorten your variable names (just kidding!).

With everything around us scaling to never-before-seen throughput, the limiting element in all this is bound to be us, the human users, and the organizations we work in. One may wonder, then, why scaling and optimizing throughput in organizations is considered a very different field from scaling software systems, mostly ignored by the IT architects who know so much about scalability. I may have become an Architect Astronaut[82] suffering from Oxygen deprivation due to exceedingly high levels of abstraction, but I can't help but feel that many of the scalability and performance approaches known to experienced IT architects can just as well be applied to scaling organizations. If a *Coffee Shop* (8) can teach us about maximizing a system's throughput, maybe our knowledge of IT systems design can help improve an organization's performance?

Component Design - Personal Productivity

Increasing throughput starts with the individual. Some folks are simply ten times more productive than others. For me it's hit or miss: when I am "in the zone", I can be incredibly productive but lose traction just as quickly when I am being frequently interrupted or annoyed by something. So I won't bestow you with any great personal advice, but instead refer you to the many resources like GTD - Getting Things Done[83], which advise you to minimize inventory of open tasks (making the "lean" folks happy) and to break down large tasks into smaller ones that are immediately actionable. For example, "I really ought to replace that old clunker" turns into "visit 3 dealerships this weekend". Incoming stuff is categorized and either immediately processed or parked until it's actionable, thus reducing the number of concurrent threads. The suggestions are very sound, but as always it takes a bit of trust and lots of discipline to succeed at implementing them.

---

[82]http://www.joelonsoftware.com/articles/fog0000000018.html
[83]https://en.wikipedia.org/wiki/Getting_Things_Done

Avoid Sync Points - Meetings Don't Scale

Let's assume people individually do their best to be productive and have high throughput, meaning we have efficient and effective system components. Now we need to look at the integration architecture, which defines the interaction between components, i.e. people. One of the most common interaction points (short of e-mail, more on that later) surely is the *meeting*. The name alone gives some of us goose bumps because it suggests that people get together to "meet" each other, but doesn't define any specific agenda, objective, or outcome.

From a systems design perspective meetings have another troublesome property: they require multiple humans to be (mostly) in the same place at the same time. In software architecture, we call this a "synchronization point", widely known as one of the biggest throughput killers. The word "synchronous" derives from Greek and essentially means things happening at the same time. In distributed systems for things to happen at the same time, some components have to wait for others, which is quite obviously not the way to maximize throughput.

The longer the wait for the synchronization point, the more dramatic the negative impact on performance becomes. In some organizations finding a meeting time slot among senior people can take a month or longer. Such resource contention on people's time significantly slows down decision-making and project progress (and hurts *Economies of Speed* (31)). The effect is analog to locking database updates: if many processes are trying to update the same table record, throughput suffers enormously as most processes just wait for others to complete, eventually ending up in the dreaded *deadlock*. Administrative teams in large organizations acting as *transaction monitor* underlines the overhead caused by using meetings as the primary interaction model. Worse yet, full schedules cause people to start blocking time "just in case", a form of *pessimistic resource allocation*, which has exactly the opposite of the intended effect on the *System Behavior* (10).

While getting together can be useful for brainstorming, critical discussions, or decisions (see below), the worst kind of meetings must be status meetings. If someone wants to know where a project "stands", why would they want to wait for the next status meeting that takes place in a week or two? To top it off, many status meetings I attended had someone read text off a document that wasn't distributed ahead of the meeting lest someone read through it and escapes the meeting.

Interrupts Interrupt - Phone Calls

When you can't wait for the next meeting, you tend to call the person. I know well as I log half a dozen incoming calls a day, which I routinely don't answer (they typically lead to an e-mail starting with the phrase "I was unable to reach you by phone", whose purpose I never quite understood). Phone calls have short wait times when compared to meetings, but are still synchronous and thus require all resources to be available at the same time. How many times have you played "phone tag" where you were unable to answer a call just to experience the reverse when you call back? I am not sure there's an analog to this in system communication (I should know; after all, I am documenting Conversation Patterns[84]), but it's difficult to imagine this as effective communication.

Phone calls are "interrupts" (they are blockable by muting your ringer), and in an open environment they not only interrupt you but also your coworkers. That's one reason that Google Japan's engineering desks were by default not equipped with phones - you had to specifically request one, which was looked upon as a little old-fashioned. The damage ringing phones can do in open office spaces was already illustrated in Tom DeMarco and Tim Lister's classic *Peopleware*[85]. The "tissue trick" won't work anymore with

---

[84]http://www.eaipatterns.com/patterns/conversation
[85]DeMarco, Lister: Peopleware: Productive Projects and Teams (3rd Edition), Addison-Wesley , 2013

digital phones, but luckily virtually all of them have a volume setting. My pet peeve related to phones is people busting into my office while I am talking on the speaker phone, so I'd like to build a pet project to illuminate an "on air" sign while I am on the phone.

Piling on instead of backing off

Retrying an unsuccessful operation is a typical remote conversation pattern. It's also a dangerous operation because it can escalate a small disturbance in a system into an onslaught of retries, which brings everything to a grinding halt. That's why Exponential Back-off[86] is a well-known pattern and forms the basis of many low-level networking protocols, such as the CSMA/CD (Carrier Sense, Multiple Access with Collision Detection), which is a core element of the Ethernet protocol.

Ironically, humans tend to not back off if a phone call fails, but have a tendency to "pile on": if you don't pick up, they tend to call you at ever shorter intervals to signal that "it's urgent". Ultimately, they will back off, but only after burdening the system with overly aggressive retries. Such behavior contributes to uneven resource utilization. It seems that either everyone seems to be calling you or it's extremely quiet. Asynchronous communication with queues in contrast can perform "traffic shaping" – spikes are absorbed by the queue, allowing the "service" to process requests at the optimal rate without becoming overloaded.

Asynchronous Communication - Email, Chat, and More

In corporate environments, E-Mail tends to draw almost as much ire as meetings. It has one big advantage, though: it's asynchronous. Instead of being interrupted, you can process your e-mail whenever

---

[86]https://en.wikipedia.org/wiki/Exponential_backoff

you have a few minutes to spare. Getting a response may take slightly longer, but it's a classic "throughput over latency" architecture, best described by Clemens Vaster's analogy of building wider bridges, not faster cars, to solve the perennial congestion on the 2-lane floating bridge that's part of Washington State Route 520 between Seattle and Redmond.

E-mail also has drawbacks, the main one being people flooding everyone's inbox because the perceived cost of sending mail is zero. You must have a good inbox filter if you want to survive. Also, mail isn't collectively searchable – each person has their own record of history. I guess you could call that an *eventually-consistent* architecture of sorts and just live with it, but it still seems horribly inefficient. I wonder how many copies of that same 10 MB PowerPoint presentation plus all its prior versions are stored on a typical Exchange server.

Integrating chat with e-mail can overcome some of these limitations: if you don't get a reply or the reply indicates that a real-time discussion is needed, the "reply by chat" button turns the conversation into quasi-synchronous mode: it still allows the receiver to answer at will (so it's asynchronous), but allows for much quicker iterations than mail. Products like Slack, which favor a chat / channel paradigm, also enable asynchronous communication without e-Mail. Systems architects would liken this approach to *tuple spaces*, which, based on a *blackboard* architectural style, are well suited for scalable, distributed systems thanks to loose coupling and avoiding duplication.

Speaking of blackboard, the most transformative change in corporate collaboration I have seen was the advent of Google Docs and it isn't due to my 7 years of drinking Google Kool-Aid. In fact, when Docs first became available internally at Google, I complained a lot because its feature maturity was well below that of Microsoft Word 5.0. However, being able to collaborate in real-time on a document completely changed the way people work together towards a shared outcome. Having had to go back to mailing Word documents back-

and-forth has been an extremely frustrating experience.

Asking Doesn't Scale - Build a Cache!

Much of corporate communication consists of asking questions, often via synchronous communication. This doesn't scale because the same questions get asked again and again. Architects would surely introduce a cache into their system to offload the source component, especially when they receive repeated requests for basic information, such as a photo of a new team member. In such cases, I simply type the person's name into Google and reply with a hyperlink to an on-line picture, asking Google instead of another person.

Search scales, but only if the answers are available in a searchable medium. Therefore, if you receive a question, reply so that everyone can see (and search) the answer, e.g. on an internal forum – that's how you load the cache. Taking the time to explain something in a short document or forum post scales: 1000 people can search for and read what you have to share. 1000 1:1 meetings to explain the same story would take half of your annual work time.

One cache killer I have experienced is the use of different templates, which aim for efficiency, but hurt data reuse. For example, when I answer requests for my resume with a link to Google or LinkedIn, I observe a human transcribing the data found on-line into a prescribed Word template. Some things are majorly wrong in the digital universe.

Poorly Set Domain Boundaries - Excessive Alignment

While some communication styles may scale better than others, all will ultimately collapse under heavy traffic because humans can only handle so much throughput, even in chat or asynchronous communication. The goal therefore mustn't only be to tune communication but also to reduce it. Large corporations suffer from a lot of unnecessary communication, caused for example by the need "to align". I often jest that "aligning" is what I do when my car doesn't run straight or wears the tires unevenly. Why I need to do it at work all the time puzzled me. Especially as "alignment" invariably triggered a meeting with no clear objective (see above).

In corp speak, "to align" means to coordinate on an issue and come to some sort of common understanding or agreement. A common understanding is an integral part of productive teamwork, but what worries me is that the act of "aligning" takes on a life of its own. My suspicion is that it's a sign of mis-alignment (pun intended) between the project and organizational structures: the people that are critical to a project's success or are vital decision makers aren't part of the project, requiring frequent "steering" and "alignment" meetings. The system design analog for this problem is setting domain boundaries poorly, drawing on Eric Evan's Domain-driven Design[87] concept of a Bounded Context[88]. Slicing a distributed system across poorly set domain boundaries is almost guaranteed to increase latency and burden the system.

Self-Service is Better Service

Self-service generally has poor connotations: if the price was the same, would you rather eat at McDonald's or in a white table-cloth restaurant with waiter service? If you are a food chain looking to optimize throughput, though, would you rather be McDonald's or the quaint Italian place with 5 tables? Self-service scales.

Requesting a service or ordering a product by making a phone call or e-mailing spreadsheet attachments for someone to manually enter data doesn't scale, even if you lower the labor cost with near- or offshoring. In order to scale, *automate everything* (14): make all

---

[87]https://domainlanguage.com/
[88]http://martinfowler.com/bliki/BoundedContext.html

functions and processes available on-line on the intranet, ideally both as Web UIs and as (access protected) service API's so users can layer new services or custom user interfaces on top, e.g. to combine popular functions.

Staying Human

Does scaling organizations like computer systems mean that the digital world shuns personal interaction, turning us into faceless e-mail and workflow drones that must maximize throughput? I don't think so. I very much value personal interaction for brainstorming, negotiation, solution finding, bonding, or just having a good time. That's what we should maximize face-to-face time for. Having someone read slides aloud or calling me the third time to ask the same question could be achieved many times faster by optimizing communication patterns. Am I being impatient? Possibly, but in a world where everything moves faster and faster, patience may not be the best strategy. High-throughput systems don't reward patience.

27. Slow Chaos is not Order

Going fast? Bring Discipline!

Agile or just fast? The next turn will tell.

Everyone has their "pet peeves" or "hot buttons", things that you've heard often enough that even though they may be trivial, they really annoy you. In private life, these issues tend to revolve around things like toothpaste tubes: cap off vs. cap on or squeezed from the bottom vs. from the middle. Such differences have been known to put numerous marriages and live-in relationships in danger (hint: a second tube runs about $1.99).

In the corporate IT world, pet peeves tend to be related to things more technical in nature. Mine is people using the word "agile" without having understood its meaning, some 15 years after the Agile Manifesto[89] was authored. Surely you have overheard conversations like the following:

---

[89]http://agilemanifesto.org

- What's your next major deliverable? Dunno - we are *agile*!
- What's your project plan? Because we are *agile*, we are so fast that we couldn't keep the plan up-to-date!
- Could I see your documentation? Don't need it - we are *agile*!
- Could you tell me about your architecture? Nope - *agile* projects don't need this!

Such ignorance is only topped by statements that agile methods aren't suited for your company or department because they are too chaotic for such a structured environment. Ironically, the opposite is usually the case: corporate environments often lack the discipline to implement agile processes.

Fast vs. agile

My first annoyance about the widespread abuse of the word "agile" is repeatedly having to remind people that the method is called "agile", not "fast", and for a good reason. Agile methods are about hitting the right target through frequent re-calibration and embracing change rather than trying to predict the environment and eliminating uncertainty. Firing from afar at a moving target is fast, but not agile - you will likely miss. Agile methods allow course-corrections along the way, more like a guided missile (even though I am not fond of the weapons analogy). Agile gets you where you need to be quickly. Running the wrong direction faster isn't a method, but foolishness.

Speed and Discipline

When observing something that moves fast, it's easy to feel a sense of chaos: too many things are going on at the same time for someone to judge how it all really fits together. A good example is a Formula 1 pit stop: *screech - whir - whir - roar*, and the car has four new tires in under four seconds (refueling is no longer allowed in F1 racing).

Watching this process at full speed leaves one slightly dizzy and feeling that it's some sort of miracle or in fact a bit chaotic. You'll have to watch the procedure a few times, ideally in slow motion, to appreciate that few things are more disciplined than a pit stop crew: every movement is precisely choreographed and trained hundreds of times. After all, at F1 speed a second longer in the pit means lagging almost 100 meters behind.

Moving fast in the IT world likewise requires discipline. Automated tests are your safety belt - how else would you be able to deploy code into production at moment's notice, e.g. in case of a serious problem? The most *valuable* time for an on-line retailer to deploy code is right in the holiday season, when customer traffic is at its peak. Because that's when a critical fix or a new feature can have the biggest positive impact on the bottom line. Ironically, that's exactly the time when most corporate IT shops have a "frozen zone", which forbids deploying any code changes. Making a code push in peak traffic takes confidence. Having iron discipline and lots of practice can make you more confident and fast. Fear will slow you down. Confidence without discipline will make you crash and burn.

Fast and Good

Agile development overcomes the perception that things are either fast or of high quality by *adding a new dimension* (36). This admittedly makes it difficult to really grasp the concept without seeing it in action. I often claim that "agile cannot be taught, it can only be shown", meaning that you should learn agile methods by working in an agile team, not from a textbook.

I describe the attributes required for fast software development and deployment (often referred to as "DevOps") as follows:

- Development *velocity* assures that you can make code changes swiftly. If the code base is fraught with technical debt, such as duplication, you will lose speed right there.

- Once you made a code change, you must have the *confidence* in your code's correctness, e.g. through code reviews, rigorous automated tests, and small, incremental releases. If you lack confidence, you will hesitate and you can't be fast.
- Deployment must be *repeatable*, usually by being 100% automated. All your creativity should go into writing great features for your users, not into making each deployment work. Once you decide to deploy, you must depend on the deployment working exactly as it did the last 100 times.
- Your run-time must be *elastic* because once your users like what you built, you must be able to handle the traffic.
- You need *feedback* from monitoring to make sure you can spot production issues early and to learn what your users need. If you don't know in which direction to head, moving faster is no help.
- And last but not least you need to *secure* your run-time environment against accidental and malicious attacks, especially when deploying new features frequently, which may contain, or rely on libraries that contain, security exploits.

In unison, such a process makes for a disciplined, but fast-moving and agile development process. People who haven't seen such a process live often cannot quite believe how liberating working with confidence is. Even with the 15-year-old build system for my eaipatterns.com web site I don't hesitate for a second to delete all build artifacts to rebuild and redeploy them from scratch.

Slow-moving Chaos

If high speed requires high discipline (or ends up in certain disaster), is it true then that slow speed allows sloppiness? While not logically equivalent, the reality shows that this is usually the case. Once you look under the cover of traditional processes, you realize that there's a lot of messiness, rework, and uncontrolled *black markets* (25). For example, US auto plants in the 1980s apparently dedicated up to one-quarter of the floor space to rework[90]. No wonder Japanese car companies came in and ate their lunch with a disciplined, zero-defect approach, which acknowledged that stopping a production line to debug a problem is more effective than churning out faulty cars. These manufacturing companies were disrupted 30 years ago much in the same way digital companies are disrupting slow and chaotic service businesses now. Hopefully, you can learn something from their mistakes!

Alarmingly, you can find the same level of messiness in corporate IT: why would it take two weeks to provision a virtualized server? For once, because *most time is spent in queues* (31) and second, because of "thorough testing". Hold on, why would one need to test a virtual server that should be provisioned in a 100% automated and repeatable fashion? And why would it take two weeks? Usually because the process being followed isn't actually 100% automated and repeatable: a little duct tape is added here, a little optimization is made over there, a little script is edited, and someone forgot to mount the storage volumes. Oops. That's one reason to *never send a human to do a machine's job* (14).

Once you look under the veil of "proven processes", you quickly discover chaos, defined as a state of confusion or disorder. It's just so slow moving that you have to look a few times to notice it. A good way to test for chaos is to request precise documentation of aforementioned proven processes: most of the time it doesn't exist, is outdated, or not meant to be shared. Yeah, right...

ITIL to the Rescue?

If you challenge IT operations about slow chaos, you are likely to receive a stare of disbelief and a reference to ITIL[91], a proprietary

---

[90]Roberts: The Modern Firm: Organizational Design for Performance and Growth, Oxford University Press, 2007

[91]https://www.axelos.com/best-practice-solutions/itil

but widely adopted set of practices for IT service management. ITIL provides common vocabulary and structure, which can be of huge value when supplying services or interfacing with service providers. ITIL is also a bit daunting, consisting of five volumes of some 500 pages each.

When an IT organization refers to ITIL, I wonder how large the gap between perception and reality is. Do they really follow ITIL, or is it used as a shield against further investigation into the slow chaos? A few quick tests give valuable hints: I ask a sysadmin which ITIL process he or she primarily follows. Or I ask an IT manager to show me the strategic analysis of the customer portfolio described in section 4.1.5.4 of the volume on service strategy. I also prominently display a set of ITIL manuals in my office to thwart anyone's temptation of hand-waving their way through the conversation. ITIL itself is a very useful collection of service management practices. However, just like placing a math book under your pillow didn't get you an A-grade in school, referencing ITIL alone doesn't repel slow chaos.

Objectives and Discipline

Ironically, I have observed that result-oriented objectives can trigger a lack of discipline. A large data center migration project once set a clear goal of migrating a certain number of applications into a new data center location, a quite sensible objective. Alas, the provider had difficulties reliably provisioning servers in the new data center, causing many migration issues. I suggested to create an automated test that repeatedly places orders for servers in a variety of configurations and validates that all servers are delivered to spec within the promised time window. Once reliable provisioning was proven, we would start application migration. The project manager exclaimed in dread that then they'll never migrate a single application in ten years! The team was subsequently instructed to migrate applications using all means, knowing that there were significant quality issues with the servers.

Setting output-oriented objectives therefore requires an agreed-upon discipline as a baseline for achieving these objectives. This is why the *Prussian _Auftragstaktik* (23) depended on active discipline: increasing an organization's discipline allows for more far-reaching, and meaningful, objectives to be set.

The Way Out

"How come no one cleans up the slow chaos?", you may ask. Many traditional, but successful organizations simply *have too much money* (34) to really notice or bother. They must first realize that the world has changed from pursuing economies of scale to pursuing *Economies of Speed* (31). Speed is a great forcing function for automation and discipline. For most situations besides dynamic scaling, it's OK if provisioning a server takes a day. But if it takes more than 10 minutes, you know there'll be the temptation to perform a piece of it manually. And that's the dangerous beginning of slow-moving chaos. Instead, let *software eat the world* (15) and *don't send humans to do a machine's job* (14). You'll be fast and disciplined.

28. Governance Through Inception

I am from headquarters; I am here to help you.

Corporate Governance anno 1984

Corporate IT tends to have its own vocabulary. The top contender for the most frequently used word must be *to align*, which translates vaguely into having a meeting with no particular objective beyond mulling over a topic and coming to some sort of agreement short of an official approval. Large IT organizations tend to be *slowed down* (26) by doing this a lot.

After "alignment", "governance" likely comes in second. It describes harmonization and standardization across the organization by means of rules, guidelines, and standards. IT harmonization done well increases purchasing power through economies of scale. It also reduces operational costs and boosts IT security by eliminating unnecessary diversity.

While pursuing harmonization is a rather worthwhile goal, "governance" can also do harm, for example by converging on a lowest common denominator, which in the end doesn't meet the business' need. The folks setting the standards not having the necessary skill set and context is another common scenario. Worse yet, these teams may not receive sufficient feedback whether the standard is in fact working well: especially in large IT organizations top decision makers often don't use the very tools they standardize or manage - they *rarely use the standard workplace or HR tools* (25), for example.

Exerting governance in an existing organization or one that grew by acquisition involves migrating from the "wrong" system implementation to the "standard". Such migrations involve cost and risk without an apparent benefit for the local entity, which makes enforcement difficult. The enemy of governance is the "shadow IT", which describes local development outside of the reaches of central governance.

Setting Standards

Corporate governance typically starts by defining a set of standards that are to be adhered to. A standards organization will define and administer these standards, decreeing for example that product *ABC* shall be used for e-mailing and product *XYZ* for databases.

Standards have an enormous value, as epitomized by the devastating 1904 fire in Baltimore, which left many firemen from surrounding cities standing idle because their fire hose connections wouldn't fit Baltimore's fire hydrants. The National Fire Protection Association was quick to learn from this and established a standard for fire hose connections in 1905, still known as the *Baltimore Standard*.

The primary economic argument for standards is based on compatibility standards, specifications that allow interchangeability of parts, such as fire hoses and hydrants. In an IT environment, such standardization would be equivalent to standardizing interfaces rather than products, for example standardizing on SMTP, the Simple Mail Transfer Protocol, for mail transfer as opposed to Microsoft Outlook as the mail client. Compatibility standards bring flexibility and *network effects*: as many elements are able to interconnect, the benefit to all participants increases. The Internet, originally based on the HTML and HTTP standards for content and connectivity, is the perfect example. It also highlights one more time that *lines are more interesting than boxes* (22).

Enterprises must therefore articulate their main driver behind setting standards: standardizing vendor products aims to reduce cost and complexity through economies of scale, while compatibility or connectivity standards boost flexibility and innovation. Both are useful, but call for different types of standards.

For any standard to be meaningful, it needs to be based on a *well-defined vocabulary* (16) that specifies the scope of the standard. For example, the Baltimore fire hydrant standard distinguishes *pumper connections* from *fire hose connections*, specifying different diameters and thread designs. Likewise, in the IT world standards for "database", "application server", or "integration" run the risk of being meaningless without a distinction of the types of databases or servers that are to be considered.

Governance by Decree

Enforcing standards can be a bit like herding cats, even when the economic value is blatantly obvious. For example, almost one hundred years after the Baltimore standard, fighting large fires such as the Oakland Hills Fire of 1991 is still impeded by cities not following the standard[92]. Often, the deviation from the standard is a historical artifact or purposely driven by vendors to gain lock-in.

In many organizations, a diagnostic "police" will visit different entities to ascertain their standard compliance, which gives rise to the joke about the biggest lie in a corporate environment: "I am from headquarters; I am here to help you." Cyber-security can be a useful vehicle to drive standardization: non-standard or outdated versions of software generally carry a higher risk of vulnerability than well-maintained, harmonized environments.

A specific challenge is posed by users who *also* use a standard, in addition to their own solution. They thus correctly proclaim "yes, we do drive BMW cars" in line with the (fictitious) corporate standard while the parking lot is full of Mercedes, Rolls-Royce, and Yugos. A second phenomenon has users employ the standard, but for the wrong purpose. For example, they may use the standard BMW, but as a meeting room for 4 people and not to actually drive anywhere (they prefer Mercedes for that). Sounds absurd? I have seen lots of examples similarly absurd in corporate IT!

Governance through infrastructure

Interestingly, in my 7 years at Google no one ever mentioned the word "governance" (or "SOA" or "Big Data" for that matter). Knowing that Google not only has a fantastic service architecture and world-leading big data analytics, one might guess then that they also have strong governance. In fact, Google has an extremely strong governance in places where it matters most, for example run-time infrastructure. You were free to write your code in emacs, vi, Notepad, IntelliJ, Eclipse or any other editor, but there was basically only one way to deploy software to the production infrastructure, on one kind of operating system (in the old days, you could choose between 32 or 64 bit), on one kind of hardware.

---

[92]Seck, Evans: Major U.S. Cities Using National Standard Fire Hydrants, One Century After the Great Baltimore Fire, NISTIR 7158, National Institute of Standards and Technology

While occasionally painful, this strictness worked because most software developers would put up with pretty much anything to have their software run on a Google-scale infrastructure: it was, and likely still is, a decade ahead of what most other companies were using. The governance didn't need to take the form of a decree because the system was vastly superior to anything else, rendering not following it a guaranteed waste of time. If the corporate car is a Ferrari or has a Flux Capacitor for time travel[93], people won't be running to the VW dealer. In Google's case, the Flux Capacitor was the amazing "Borg" deployment and machine management system, which has been publicly described in a Google research paper[94]. For Google the system's economies of scale worked so well that in the end it became reasonable to have everyone drive a Ferrari while enjoying the fast pace.

Netflix exerts governance over application design and architecture by running their infamous *chaos monkey* against deployed software to verify that the software is resilient and immune against failure propagation, e.g. by using *circuit breakers*[95]. Non-compliant software will be pummeled in production by automated compliance testers. Hardly any organization that brags about their corporate governance group would have the guts to do the same.

Inception

In large IT organizations the motivation is generally a little less pronounced and the infrastructure (cough!) a little less advanced. Who has been to the movies in recent years must have come across *Inception*, an ingenious Christopher Nolan flick depicting corporate criminals who steal trade secrets from their victim's subconscious. The title derives from the storyline that the team usually operates in "read only" mode to extract secrets from the victim's memory,

---

[93]A reference to the 80s movie *Back to the Future*
[94]http://research.google.com/pubs/pub43438.html
[95]Nygard: Release It!: Design and Deploy Production-Ready Software; Pragmatic Bookshelf, 2007

but that for their big coup they have to actively implant an idea into a victim's mind to cause him to take a particular action – a process referred to "inception". In the movie the tricky part is to make the victim truly believe it was his idea.

If we could perform inception, corporate governance would be a lot easier: IT units would independently come to the conclusion to use the same software. This isn't quite as absurd as it sounds because there's one magic ingredient in today's IT world that makes it possible: change. With change comes the need to update systems (still have Lotus Notes somewhere?) and the opportunity to set new standards without any additional migration costs. You "simply" have to agree on which incarnation of the new piece of technology you want to employ, for example for a software-defined network, a big data cluster, or an on-premise platform-as-a-service. That you have to do by inception.

Inception in corporate IT works only if the governing body is ahead of the rest of the world, so they can set the direction before the widespread need arises. Acting as an educator, they supply new ideas to their audience and can inject, or incept, ideas, such as demand for a specific product or standard. In a sense, that's what marketing has been doing for centuries: creating demand for the product that manufacturing happened to have built.

In times of change, the "new" will ultimately replace the "old" and through constant inception the landscape becomes more standardized. The key requirement is that "central" has to innovate faster than the business units so that when a division realizes they want a big data analytics cluster, corporate IT already has clear guidance and a reference implementation. Doing so requires foresight and funding, but beats chasing business units for non-compliance and facing migration costs.

Emperor's new Clothes

Traditional IT governance can also cause an awkward scenario best described as the *Emperor's New Clothes*: a central team develops a product that exists primarily in slide decks, so-called *vaporware*. When such a product is decreed as a standard, which is essentially meaningless, customers may happily adopt it because it's an easy way to earn a "brownie point", or even funding, for standard compliance without the need for much actual implementation. In the end everyone appears happy, except the shareholders: it's a giant and senseless waste of energy.

Governance through Necessity

In an interesting book about refugee camps in the Western Sahara[96] I learned that almost everyone in these camps drives the same model of car, either a Land Rover all-terrain vehicle or an older Mercedes sedan. Together, these models make up for over 90% of all cars and 85% of sedans are Mercedes – a corporate governor's wild dream! How come? Residents chose an inexpensive and very reliable car that could withstand the rough terrain and heat. The standardization came through simple necessity, though: buying another model of car would mean not being able to take advantage of the existing skill set and the pool of spare parts. In an environment of economic constraints, these are major considerations. Corporate IT has the same forces, especially regarding IT skill set availability for new technologies. The observed diversity in corporate environments is therefore a *Rich Company* (34) problem: the scarcity of skills or resources just isn't strong enough to drive joint decision making – they can easily be solved with more money. One could also argue that the refugee camps had the advantage of a so-called "green field" installation, even though that term seems awfully inappropriate for people being displaced in the desert.

---

[96]Herz: From Camp to City: Refugee Camps of the Western Sahara; Lars Muller, 2012

Transformation

Bringing change into large organizations is rewarding but challenging – you'll need everything you learned so far to tackle this ultimate challenge. You must first understand how a complex organization works before you can undertake to change it. Your architectural thinking will help you understand organizations as complex systems. Superb communication skills help you garner support while leadership skills are needed to effect a lasting change. Lastly, your IT architect skills allow you to implement the necessary technical changes necessary for the organization to work in a different way.

Citing *The Matrix* one more time (after all, Neo is quite a change agent in a tough environment!), the exchange between *The Architect* and *The Oracle* draws the apt context:

> The Architect: You played a very dangerous game.

> The Oracle: Change always is.

Interestingly, in *The Matrix* the Architect is the main entity trying to prevent change. You should identify yourself with Neo instead, making sure to have an Oracle to back you up.

Not all Change is Transformation

Not every change deserves to be called *transformation*. You can change the layout of the furniture in your living room, but you *transform* (or maybe convert) your house into a club, retail store, or place of worship. The Latin origin of the word *trans-form* means changing shape or structure. When we speak of IT Transformation we therefore imply not an incremental evolution, but a fundamental restructuring of the technology landscape, the organizational setup, and the culture. Basically, expect to have to turn the house upside down, cut it into pieces, and put it back together in a new shape. As an architect you are best qualified to understand how technical and organizational changes depend on each other so you can solve the Gordian knot of interdependencies.

Bursting the Boiler

A prevalent risk in corporate transformation agendas is upper management recognizing the need for change and subsequently applying pressure to the organization, e.g. to become faster, more agile, more customer-centric, etc. However, the organization, and especially middle management, is often not ready to transform and attempts to achieve the targets set by upper management within the old way of working. This can put enormous strain on the organization and is unlikely to meet the ambitions. I compare this to a steam engine, which is surpassed by a fast electric train. In an attempt to speed up, the operator may throw more coals onto the fire to increase the boiler pressure. Unfortunately, this will burst the boiler rather than beat the electric train. As an architect you have to devise a new engine that can keep up instead of simply turning up the dials.

Why me?

As an architect you may think: "Why me? Isn't this where the high-paid consultants come in?" They can certainly help, but you can't just inject change from the outside; it must come from the inside. This is one reason why I am doing transformation not as a consultant, but as a full-time employee, even though it has some challenges (see *Fifty Shades of IT* (1)).

Triggering a change in technology or development approaches also requires you to take a role in changing the organization: you can't be agile or use a DevOps development style if you don't adjust the organization and its culture.

To affect lasting change in an organization you need to understand:

- That organizations *Will not change if there's no pain* (29).
- How to *Lead Change* (30) by showing a better way of doing things.
- Why organizations need to think in *Economies of Speed* (31) instead of Economies of Scale.
- Why an *Infinite Loop* (32) is an essential part of digital organizations.
- Why excessively *Buying IT services* (34) can be a fallacy.
- How to speed up organizations by *Spending less Time Standing in Line* (35).
- How you can get the organization to *Think in New Dimensions* (36).

29. No Pain, no Change!

And watching late night TV does not help...

Go, go, gooooo!

A colleague of mine once attended a "digital showcase" event in his company, which highlighted many innovative projects and external hackathons the company had organized. Upon returning to his desk, though, he found himself in the same old corporate IT world where he is forced to clock time, cannot get a server in less than 3 weeks, and isn't allowed to install software on his laptop. He was wondering whether he was caught in some twisted incarnation of two-speed IT, but that made little sense as his project was part of the fast-moving "digital" speed.

Stages of Transformation

I had a different answer: transformation is a difficult and time-consuming process that doesn't happen overnight. People just don't wake up one day and behave completely differently, no matter how many TED Talks they listened to the day before. A talk I once attended illustrated how difficult it is to change which part of the body you dry first with your towel after taking a shower in the morning. I guess the speaker was right - I never changed that.

To illustrate the stages a person or an organization tends to go through when transforming their habits, I drew up the example of someone changing from eating junk food to leading a healthy lifestyle. With no scientific evidence, I quickly came up with 10 stages:

1. You eat junk food. Because it's tasty.
2. You realize eating junk food is bad for you. But you keep eating it. Because it is tasty.
3. You start watching late-night TV weight-loss programs. While eating junk food. Because it is so tasty.
4. You order a miracle-exercise machine from the late-night TV program. Because it looked so easy.
5. You use the machine a few times. You realize that it's hard work. Worse yet, no visible results were achieved during the two weeks you used it. Out of frustration you eat more junk food.
6. You force yourself to exercise even though it's hard work and results are meager. Still eating some junk food.
7. You force yourself to eat healthier, but find it not tasty.
8. You actually start liking vegetables and other healthy food.
9. You become addicted to exercise. Your motivation changed from losing weight to doing what you truly like.
10. Friends ask you for advice on how you did it. You have become a source of inspiration to others.

Change happens incrementally and takes a lot of time plus dedication.

Digital Transformation Stages

Drawing the analogy between my colleague's company and my freshly created framework, I concluded that they must be somewhere between stage 3 and 4 on their transformation journey. What he attended was the digital equivalent of watching late-night miracle solutions. Maybe the company even invested in or acquired one of the nifty start-ups, which are young, hip, and use DevOps. But upon returning to his desk, he experienced that the organization was still eating lots of junk food.

I suggest that the transformation scale from 1 to 10 isn't linear: the critical steps occur from stage 1 to 2 (awareness, not to be underestimated!), 5 to 6 (overcoming disillusionment) and from 7 to 8 (wanting instead of forcing yourself). I would therefore give his company a lot of credit for starting the journey, but warn them that disillusionment is likely to lie ahead.

Wishful Thinking Sells Snake Oil

It can be amazing how gullible smart individuals and organizations become when they are presented with miracle claims for a better life. Once people or organizations have entered stage 3, whole industries that are built on selling "snake oil" eagerly await them, overweight individuals and slow-paced corporate IT departments alike: late-night weight loss commercials and shiny demos showing business people building cloud solutions in no time. As Russel Ackoff once pointedly put it: *Managers are incurably susceptible to panacea peddlers. They are rooted in the belief that there are simple, if not simple-minded, solutions to even the most complex of problems* (from A Lifetime of Systems Thinking[97]). When you are looking for a quick change, it's difficult to resist, especially if you don't have your own *World Map* (13).

[97]https://thesystemsthinker.com/a-lifetime-of-systems-thinking

Digital natives have it easy because, as the name suggests, they were born on the upper levels of the digital transformation scale and never had to make it through this painful change process. Others feel the pain and tend to search for an easy way out. The problem is that this approach will never get you beyond stage 5, where real change hasn't happened yet.

Tuning the engine

Not everyone who buys snake oil is a complete fool, though. Many organizations adopt worthwhile practices but don't understand that these practices don't work outside of a specific context. For example, sending a few hundred managers to become Scrum Master certified doesn't make you agile. You need to change the way people think and work and establish new values. Holding a stand-up meeting every day that resembles a status call where people report 73% progress also doesn't transform your organization. It's not that stand-up meetings are a bad idea, rather the opposite, but they are about much more than standing up[98]. Real transformation has to go far beyond scratching the surface and change the system.

Systems theory (10) teaches us that to change the observed behavior of a system, you must change the system itself. Everything else is wishful thinking. It's like wanting to improve the emissions of a car by blocking the exhaust pipe. If you want a cleaner running car, there's no other way than going all the way back to the engine and tuning it. When you want to change the behavior of a company, you need to go to its engine – the people and the way they are organized. This is the burdensome, but only truly effective way.

Help along the way

Most enterprise vendors do resemble the folks selling overpriced workout machines on late-night TV: their products work, but not

---

[98]http://martinfowler.com/articles/itsNotJustStandingUp.html

quite as advertised and they are in fact overpriced. A good walk in the park every day likely produces the same results for free. You just have to be smart enough to know that and disciplined enough to stick to it.

Many enterprise IT vendors provide genuine innovation to their customers, but also benefit from corporate IT being unable to fully transform themselves. As I once stated in a slightly exaggerated way: "Corporate IT tends to pay for its stupidity. If you are stupid, you better be rich!" Rhetoric aside, I place enterprise vendors on a scale ranging from "old school" via "selling the new world to old enterprises" to "truly new world". My goal is to build sufficient internal skill to use products as far to the right as possible. An organization that doesn't have the skill yet pays "learning money", a concept well-known in German as *Lehrgeld*. If spending the money helps them do better next time, it's a good investment. As always, I make sure to *document such decisions* (9).

The consultants and enterprise vendors that surround traditional enterprises (see *Money can't buy love* (34)) have a limited incentive to fully transform their clients into becoming digital: digital companies tend to shun consultants and largely employ open-source technology, often developed by themselves. Because externals are set to profit from the transformation path itself, they are useful in helping an enterprise start the transformation, as this brings the willingness to invest money. However, they aren't quite as keen to catapult their customers into a state where their advice or products are no longer needed. This love-hate relationship is likely to affect the role an architect plays in the transformation effort: you can't achieve it without external help, but you have to be aware that it's a co-opetition rather than true collaboration.

The Pain of not Changing

The biggest risk during the transformation journey is suffering a relapse after having bought "snake oil" just to realize that it doesn't achieve the promised results, or at least not as quickly as anticipated. This risk is particularly high at stages 4 or 5 of my model.

The inevitable pain of changing makes the lure of the easy path, i.e. not changing or abandoning half-way, a clear-and-present danger. The long-term pain of not changing is easily put aside because it isn't happening yet. Plus, you already accepted the current state, even if it clearly isn't optimal. The certainty of knowing the current state proves to be a major force against change, which carries a large amount of uncertainty – who knows whether all the projected benefits will actually materialize? It could be getting worse for all we know.

IT organizations, especially operations teams (see *Run vs. Change* (12)), tend to equate change to risk. Dangerously, this leads to the conclusion that not changing carries no risk. That's a classic fallacy and poor *decision making* (6): not changing can bear immense risks, such as security risks or losing a competitive edge. It can even cost the whole business. Ask Blockbuster Video or Kodak.

The insight that change was needed comes often much later, when the cost of not having changed becomes blatantly and painfully apparent. Sadly, at that time the list of available options tends to be much shorter, or empty. This is true for individuals ("I wish I had started a healthier life when I was young") as well as organizations ("we wish we had cleaned up our IT before we became disrupted"). When people reflect on their lives they are much more likely to regret *not* having done things as opposed to the things they did. The logical conclusion is simple: do more things and keep doing those that work well.

Getting over the Hump

A linear chain of events has one tricky property: the probability of making it through all steps computes as the product of the individual transition probabilities between each step and the next.

Let's say you are a quite determined person and have a 70% chance of making it from one step to the next, even though the machine you ordered from late-night TV didn't work quite as advertised. If you compound this probability across the 9 steps needed to go from stage 1 to stage 10, you arrive at a 4% probability, 1 in 25, of making it to the goal. If you assume a fifty-fifty chance at each step, which might be more realistic (just look on eBay for barely used exercise machines), you end up with $1/2^9 = 0.2\%$ or 1 in 512 (!). "Against all odds" comes to mind, even though it's probably not Phil Collin's best song.

The biggest enemy of change is complacency: if things aren't so bad, the motivation to change is low. Organizations can artificially increase the pain of not changing, e.g. by creating fear or conjuring a (fake) crisis before the real crisis occurs. Such a strategy can work, but is risky. It cannot be applied many times, though, as people will start ignoring the repeated "fire drill". Still, conjuring a crisis beats undergoing a real crisis. Many organizations only really start to change when they have a "near-death" experience. The problem is that near-death often results in actual death.

30. Leading Change

The island of sanity in the sea of desperation

Don't get voted off the island!

Demonstrating positive results from a different way of doing things in a small team can help overcome complacency and the fear of uncertainty, and thus is a good way to start a transformation. One shouldn't forget, though, that the "trail blazers" on such teams have a doubly tough job: they need to overcome the pain of change and do so in an environment that's still at stage 1 of the transformation journey. This is comparable to eating healthy when everyone around you at the table is having tasty cake and the restaurant has nothing healthy on the menu at all.

To succeed, you need a firm belief and perseverance. The corporate IT equivalent of trying to eat healthy at the cake party is trying to be agile when it takes 4 weeks to get a new server or when contemporary development tools and hardware aren't allowed because they violate corporate security standards. You got to be willing to swim upstream to affect change.

A tractor passing the race car

One particular danger of leading change with a different approach is that the existing, slow approaches are often more suitable for the current environment. This is a form of *Systems resisting change* (10) and can result in your fancy new software / hardware / development approach being pummeled by the old, existing ways. I compare this to building a full-fledged race car, just to find out that in your corporate environment each car has to pull 3 tons of baggage in the form of rules and regulations. And instead of a nice, paved race track, you find yourself in a foot-deep sea of process mud. You will find out that the old corporate tractor slowly but steadily passes your shiny new Formula 1 car, which is busily throwing up mud while shredding its rear tires. In such a scenario, it becomes difficult to argue that you devised a better way of doing things.

It's therefore critical to change processes and culture along with introducing new technology. A race car on a tractor pulling contest will be laughable at best. You'll have to dry up the swamp and build a proper road before it makes sense to commission a race car. You also need to employ your *Communication Skills* to secure management support when setbacks happen.

Setting course

To motivate people for change, you can either dangle the digital carrot, painting pictures of happy, digital life on far horizons, or wield the digital stick, warning of impending doom through disruption. In the end, you'll likely need a little bit of both, but the carrot is generally the more noble approach. For the carrot to work, you need to paint a tangible picture of the alternate future and set visible, measurable targets based on the company strategy.

For example, if the corporate strategy is based on increasing *speed* to reduce time-to-market, a tangible and visible goal would be to cut the release cycle for your division's software products or services in half (or more) every year. If the goal is *resilience*, you set a goal of halving average times-to-recovery for outages (setting a goal related to the number of outages has two issues: it incentivizes hiding outages and it's not the number of outages that count, but the observed downtime). If you want to add a little *stick* to that goal, deploy a *chaos monkey* (28) that verifies systems' resilience by randomly disabling components.

Venturing off the mainland

You cannot expect everyone to instantly join you on your journey, though, simply based on you telling stories about the magic land awaiting them in the far distance. You will surely find some explorers or adventurers-at-heart who are willing to get on the boat just based on your vision or charisma. Some may not even believe your promises, but simply find sailing to unknown shores more appealing than just sitting around. These folks are your early adopters and can become powerful multipliers for your mission. Find them, connect them in a community, and take them along.

Others will wait to see whether your ship actually floats. Be kind to them and pick them up for the journey once they are ready. These folks may actually be more committed as they overcame an initial hurdle or fear. Others yet will want to see you return with your ship loaded with gold. That's also fine - some have to see to believe. So you have to be patient and recruit for your transformation journey in waves.

Burning the ships

Even after folks joined you on the transformation journey, the chance of a relapse is high: on your journey you will encounter storms, pirates, sharks, sand banks, icebergs and other adverse conditions. Captains of a digital transformation have to be skilled sailors, but also strong leaders. A tough approach is to "burn the ships", derived from the story that upon arriving on a new shore the captain would burn the ships so no one can propose to retreat and go back home. I am not sure whether this approach really increases the odds of success. You want a team that's committed and believes in success as opposed to one that has doubts but no ship to return on.

The island of sanity

Some companies' change programs sail far off the mainland to overcome the constraints imposed by the old world: innovation teams move into separate buildings, use Apple hardware, run services in the Amazon Cloud, and wear hoodies. I refer to this approach as building an "island of sanity in the sea of desperation". I did exactly this in the year 2000 when our somewhat traditional consulting company vied for talent with Internet startups like WebVan and Pets.com (a plastic bag and a sock puppet decorate my private Internet Bubble archive).

Sooner or later, though, the island will become too small for the people on it, causing them to feel constrained in their career options. If the island has drifted far from the mainland because the mainland hasn't changed much at all, re-integration will be very difficult, increasing the risk that people leave the company altogether. That's what happened to most of my team in 2001. Second, people will wonder why they have to live on a small and remote island when other companies feature the same, desirable (corporate) lifestyle on their mainland. Wouldn't that seem much easier? Or, as a friend once asked, or rather challenged, me in a very pointed way: "Why don't you just quit and let them die?"

Skunkworks

Many significant innovations that came out of people working in a separate location have managed to transform the mothership, though. The best-known example perhaps is the IBM PC, which was developed far away from IBM's New York headquarters in Boca Raton, Florida. The development bypassed many corporate rules, e.g. by mostly using parts from outside manufacturers, by building an open system, or by selling through retail stores. It's hard to imagine where IBM (and the computer industry) would be without having built the PC.

IBM was certainly a company not used to moving quickly with insiders claiming that it "would take at least nine months to ship an empty box". But the prototype for the IBM PC was assembled in one month and the computer was launched only 1 year later, which required not only development, but also manufacturing setup. The team didn't circumvent all processes and for example passed the standard IBM quality assurance tests.

The IBM PC is a positive example of an ambitious but specific project being led by existing management under executive sponsorship. People working on traditional projects probably didn't feel that this project was a threat, but rather just felt that it was impossible for IBM to make a computer for less than $15,000. This approach avoided the "island" syndrome or the 2-speed IT approach where one-half of the company is "the future" and the other one the "past", which won't survive.

Local Optima

You also need to be cautious that most *Systems* (10) operate on a local optimum. While that local optimum may be extremely far removed from the much more agile and fast way digital organizations work, it's usually still better than the "surrounding" operating modes that you end up with when you make a small change to the system.

For example, an organization may only be able to push code into production every 6 months, which is a practical joke in the digital world. However, they have managed to establish processes that make this cadence workable. If you change the release cycle to 3 months, you will make people's lives worse and may hurt the product quality and even the company reputation. Hence, you should first introduce automated build and deployment tools to form the basis for faster releases. Sadly, doing so also makes the operations staff's lives worse because they are already very busy with production support and now they have to attend training and learn new tools on top. They will also make mistakes while doing so.

In your view, the organization may live on a tiny molehill while you know of a high mountain of gold somewhere else. Because you won't be able to leap straight to the mountain of gold, you first have to get them off the molehill, convincing them to keep moving after their feet get wet and muddy. That's why you must communicate a clear vision and prepare them for tougher times ahead before the new optimum can be reached.

The Valley of the Blind

One shouldn't underestimate resistance to change and innovation in large and successful enterprises that have "done things this way" for a long time. H. G. Wells' short story of the "Country of the Blind" comes to mind: an explorer falls down a steep slope and discovers a valley completely separated from the rest of the world. Unbeknownst to the explorer, a genetic disease has rendered all villagers unable to see. Upon realizing this peculiarity, the explorer feels that because "the one-eyed man is king" he can teach and rule them. However, his ability to see proves to have little advantage in a place designed for blind people without windows or lights. After struggling to take advantage of his gift, the explorer is to have his eyes removed by the village doctor to cure his strange obsessions.

Oddly, two versions of the story exist, each with a different ending: in the original version, the explorer escapes the village after struggling back up the slope. The revised version has him observe that a rock slide is about to destroy the village and he's the only one able to escape along with his blind girlfriend. In either case, it's not a happy ending for the villagers. Be careful not to fall into the "in the land of the blind, the one-eyed man is king" trap. Complex organizational systems settle into specific patterns over time and actively resist change. If you want to change the behavior, you have to change the system.

31. Economies of Speed

Death by efficiency is slow and painful

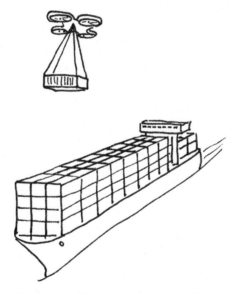

Economies of Scale vs. Economies of Speed

Large companies looking at their digital competitors are often surprised to find out that those companies don't move 10% faster, but 10x faster. A quick example shows, that even this is still quite conservative.

A large IT organization looking to define a standard for source control invested 6 months of community work to conclude that they should be using GIT. Alas, it was considered too difficult to migrate other projects off Subversion, so both products were recommended. The preparation cycle for the global architecture steering board meeting took another month, bringing the total elapsed time to 7 months or roughly 210 days.

A modern IT organization or start-up would have spent a few minutes deciding on the product and have accounts setup, a private repository created, and the first commit made in about 10 minutes. The speed-up factor comes to 210 days * (24 hours / day) * (60 minutes / hour) / 10 minutes ≈ 30,000! If that number alone doesn't scare you, keep in mind that one organization published a paper (without selecting or implementing a product such as BitBucket, GitHub, or GitLab) and is merrily dragging their legacy along. Their "decision" is thus about as meaningful as prescribing that men should wear black shoes, but brown is also allowed for historical reasons. Meanwhile the other organization is already committing code in a live repository. If you extrapolate the traditional organization's timeline to include vendor selection, license negotiation, internal alignment, paperwork, and setting up the running service, the ratio may well end up in the hundreds of thousands. Should they be scared? Yes!

Old Economies of Scale

How can this happen? Traditional organizations pursue economies of scale, meaning they are looking to benefit from their size. Size can indeed be an advantage, as can be seen in cities: density and scale provide short transportation and communication paths, diverse labor supply, better education, and more cultural offerings. Cities grow because the socioeconomic factors scale in a superlinear fashion (a city of double the size offers more than double the socioeconomic benefits), while increases in infrastructure costs are sublinear (you don't need twice as many roads for a city twice the size). But density and size also bring pollution, risk of epidemics, and congestion problems, which ultimately limit the size of cities. Still, cities grow larger and live longer than corporate organizations. One reason lies in the fact that organizations suffer more severely from the overhead introduced by processes and control structures that are required or perceived to be required to keep a large organization in check. Geoffrey West, past president of the Santa Fe Institute, summarized this dynamic in his fascinating video conversation *Why cities keep growing, corporations and people always die, and life gets faster*[99].

In corporations, economies of scale are generally driven by the desire for efficiency: resources such as machines and people must be used as efficiently as possible, avoiding downtimes due to idling and retooling. This efficiency is often pursued by using large batch sizes: making 10000 of the same widget in one production run costs less than making 10 different batches of 1000 each. The bigger you are, the larger batches you can make, and the more efficient you become. This view is overly simplistic, though, as it ignores the cost of storing intermediate products, for example. Worse yet, it doesn't consider revenue lost by not being able to serve an urgent customer order because you are in the midst of a large production run: the organization values *resource efficiency* over *customer efficiency*.

The manufacturing business has realized this about half a century ago, resulting in most things being manufactured in small batches or in one continuous batch of highly customized products. Think about today's cars: the number of options you can order are mind boggling, causing the traditional "batch" thinking to completely fall apart: cars are essentially batches of one. With all the thinking about "lean" and "just in time" manufacturing it's especially astonishing

[99]https://www.edge.org/conversation/geoffrey_west-why-cities-keep-growing-corporations-and-people-always-die-and-life-gets

that the IT industry is often still chasing efficiency instead of speed.

 A software vendor once stated that "obviously the license cost per unit goes down if you buy more licenses". To me, this isn't obvious at all as there's no distribution cost per unit of software, aside from that very sales person sitting across the table from me. Whether 10,000 customers download one license or one customer buys 10,000 licenses should be the same, as long as the software vendor doesn't *Send Humans to do a Machine's Job* (14).

It looks like enterprise software sales still has some transformations to make. To their defense, though, one has to admit that their behavior is determined by enterprise customers still stuck in the old thought pattern: super-size it to get a better deal!

In the digital world, the limiting factor for an organization's size becomes its ability to change. While in static environments being big is an advantage thanks to economies of scale, in times of rapid change *economies of speed* win over and allow start-ups and digital native companies to disrupt much larger companies. Or as Jack Welsh famously stated: "If the rate of change on the outside exceeds the rate of change on the inside, the end is near."

Behold the Flow!

The quest for efficiency focuses on the individual production steps, looking to optimize their utilization. What's completely missing is the awareness of the production flow, i.e. the flow of a piece of work through a series of production steps. Translated into organizations, individual task optimization results in every department requiring lengthy forms to be filled out before work can begin: I have been told that some organizations require firewall changes to be requested 10 days in advance. And all too often the customer is subsequently told that some thing or another is missing from the request form and is sent back to the beginning of the line. After all, helping the customer fill out the form would be less efficient. If that reminds you of government agencies, you may get the hint that such processes aren't designed for maximum speed and agility.

Besides the inevitable frustration with such setups, they trade off *flow efficiency* for *processing efficiency*: the work stations are nicely efficient, but the customers (or products or widgets) chase from station to station, fill out a form, pick a number, and wait. *And wait* (35). And wait some more just to find out they are in the wrong line or their need cannot be processed. This is dead time that isn't measured anywhere except in the customers' blood pressure. Come to think of it, in most of these places, the people going through the flow are not customers in the true sense as they don't choose to visit this process, but are forced to. That's why you are bound to experience such setups at government offices, where you could at least argue that misguided efficiency is driven by the pursuit to preserve taxpayer money. You'll also commonly find it in IT departments that exert strong *governance* (28).

Cost of Delay

For innovation and product development processes, this type of efficiency is pure poison. While digital companies do care about resource utilization (at Google data center utilization was a CEO-level topic), their real driver is speed: time-to-market.

Traditional organizations often don't understand or underestimate the value of speed. In a joint business-IT workshop, a business owner once described that his product carries substantial revenue opportunities. At the same time, the product owner asked for a specific feature that required significant development effort, but had value only in a later stage when the product would be rolled out in another country. I quickly concluded that deferring that specific feature speeds up the initial launch and harvests the portrayed revenue opportunities sooner.

Flow-based thinking calls this concept the *cost of delay* (see the excellent book *The Principles of Product Development Flow*[100]), which must be added to the cost of development. Launching a promising product later means that you lose the opportunity to gain revenue during the time of delay. For products with large revenue upside, the cost of delay can be much higher than the cost of development, but it's often ignored. On top of avoiding the cost of delay, deferring a feature and launching sooner also allows you to learn from the initial launch and adjust your requirements accordingly. The initial launch may be an utter failure, causing the product to never be launched in the second country. By deferring this feature you avoided wasting time building something that would have never been used. Gathering more information allows you to *make a better decision* (6).

A great example of a non high-tech company that embraced economies of speed is the fashion brand *Zara*, part of the Inditex fashion empire. When the pursuit of efficiency drove most fashion retailers to outsource production to low-cost suppliers in Asia, Zara implemented a vertically integrated model and manufactured three-quarters of its clothing in Europe, which allowed it to bring new designs into stores in a matter of weeks as opposed to the industry average of 3 to 6 months. In the fast-moving fashion retail industry, speed is such a significant advantage that it made Inditex' founder the second richest man on the planet.

The Value and Cost of Predictability

How come intelligent people ignore basic economic arguments such as calculating the cost of delay? They are working in a system that favors predictability over speed. Adding a feature later, or,

---

[100]Reinertsen: The Principles of Product Development Flow: Second Generation Lean Product Development, Celeritas Publishing, 2009

worse yet, deciding later whether to add it or not may require going through lengthy budget approval processes. Those processes exist because the people who control the budget value predictability over agility. Predictability makes their lives easier because they plan the budget for the next 12-24 months, and sometimes for good reasons: they don't want to disappoint shareholders with run-away costs that unexpectedly reduce the company profit. As these teams manage cost, not opportunity, they don't benefit from an early product launch.

Chasing predictability causes another well-known phenomenon: *sandbagging*. Project and budget plans sandbag by overestimating timelines or cost in order to more easily achieve their target. Keep in mind that estimates aren't single numbers, but probability distributions: a project may have a 50 percent chance of being done in four weeks' time. If "you are lucky and all goes well" it may be done in 3 weeks, but with only a 20% likelihood. Sandbaggers pick a number far off on the other end of the probability spectrum and would estimate eight weeks for the project, giving them a greater than 95% chance of meeting the target. Worse yet, if the project happens to be done in four weeks, the sandbaggers idle for another four weeks before release to avoid having their time or budget estimates cut the next time. If a deliverable depends on a series of activities, sandbagging compounds and can extend the time to delivery enormously.

The Value and Cost of Avoiding Duplication

On the list of inefficiencies, *duplication* of work must be high up: what could be more inefficient than doing the same thing twice? That's sound reasoning, but one must also consider that avoiding duplication doesn't come for free: you have to actively de-duplicate. The primary cost involved in de-duplication is coordination: to avoid duplication you first need to detect it. In a large code base this can be done efficiently through code search. In a large organization, it usually requires "alignment" meetings, i.e. synchronization points, high up in the hierarchy, which we know to *Not Scale* (26) in both computer systems and organizations.

Evolving a widely reused resource also requires coordination because changes must be compatible with existing all systems or users. Such coordination can slow down innovation. On the flip side, modern development tools, such as automated testing, can reduce the traditional dangers of duplication. Some digital companies have even begun to explicitly favor duplication because their business environment rewards economies of speed.

How to make the Switch?

Changing from efficiency-based thinking to speed-based thinking can be difficult for organizations: after all, it's less efficient! In most people's minds being less efficient translates into wasting money. On top of that, people being idle is more visible than the damage done by missed market opportunities.

Usually, this change in attitude happens only when IT is seen as driving business opportunity instead of being a cost center. While corporate IT is stuck in a cycle of cutting cost and increasing efficiency, economies of scale will prevail, which gives the digital giants an ever-bigger lead over traditional companies that dream of becoming digital, but cannot shed their old habits.

32. The Infinite Loop

Sometimes running in circles can be productive

The corporate innovation circuit. Best lap time: unknown

In programming, an infinite loop is rarely a good thing. Unless you are Apple, Inc. and your address is *1 Infinite Loop* in Cupertino, CA. But even Apple HQ appears to be moving off the infinite loop, which is a noteworthy feat in and of itself. In poorly run organizations (not Apple!) people often make cynic remarks that they run in circles and when the desired results aren't achieved, management tells them to run faster. You surely don't want to be part of that infinite loop!

Build - Measure - Learn

There's one loop, though, that's a key element of most digital companies: the continuous learning loop. Because digital companies know well that *control is an illusion* (23), they are addicted to rapid feedback. Eric Ries eternalized this concept in his book *The*

Lean Startup[101] as the *Build - Measure - Learn* cycle: a company builds a minimum viable product and launches it into production to measure user adoption and behavior. Based on the insights from live product usage the company learns and refines the product. Jeff Sussna aptly describes the "learning" part of the cycle as "operate to learn" – the goal of operations isn't to maintain the status quo, but to deliver critical insights into making a better product.

Digital RPMs

The critical KPI for most digital companies is how much they can learn per Dollar or time unit spent, i.e. how many revolutions through the *Build - Measure - Learn* cycle they can make. The digital world has thus changed the nature of the game completely and it would be foolish at best (fatal at worst) to ignore this change.

 Taking book authoring as an example, publishing *Enterprise Integration Patterns*[102] took a year of writing, followed by some 6 months of editing and 3 months of production. While we had a feeling that the book might be a success, it wasn't until another year later that we could measure the success in actual copies sold. So, making one-half revolution from *Build* to *Measure* took about 4 years! Completing the cycle would have taken another 6 to 12 months to publish a second edition.

In comparison, I am writing this book as an eBook that's published as work-in-progress. The book sold several hundred copies before it was even done, and I received reader feedback by e-mail and Twitter almost in real time as I was writing. The same is true for many other industries: digital technology has made customer feedback immediate. This is a huge opportunity, but also a huge

---

[101]Ries: The Lean Startup, Crown Business, 2011
[102]Hohpe, Woolf: Enterprise Integration Patterns, Addison-Wesley, 2003

challenge as customers have learned to expect rapid changes based on their feedback. If I don't post an update to my book in 2 or 3 weeks, people may worry that I might have given up on writing. Luckily, I find instant feedback (comments as well as purchases) hugely motivating, so I have been far more productive in writing this book than ever before.

Adopting learning as an organization's key metric is good news for another reason. While many tasks are taken over by machines, learning how to build a product that excites users remains quite firmly in the hands of humans.

Old World Hurdles

Unfortunately, traditional companies aren't built for rapid feedback cycles. They often still separate *run from change* (12) and assume a project is done by the time it reaches production. Launching a product is about the 120 degree mark in the innovation wheel-of-fortune, so making 1/3 of a single revolution counts for nothing if your competition is on their 100th refinement.

What keeps traditional organizations from completing rapid learning cycles? Their structure as a layered hierarchy: in a fairly static, slow moving world, organizing into layers has distinct advantages: it allows a small group of people to steer a large organization without having to be involved in all details. Information that travels up is aggregated and translated for easy consumption by upper management. Such a setup works very well in large organizations but has one fundamental disadvantage, though: it's horribly slow to react to changes in the environment or to insights at the working level. It takes too much time for information to travel all the way up to make a decision because each "layer" in the organization brings communication overhead and requires a translation. Even if architects can *ride the elevator* (2), it still takes time for decisions to trickle back down through a web of budgeting and steering processes. Once again we aren't talking about a difference of 10%, but of factors in the hundreds or thousands: traditional organizations often run feedback cycles to the tune of 18 months while digital companies can do it in days or weeks.

In times where most every organization wants to become more "digital" and the technical platforms are readily available as open source or cloud services, building a fast-learning organization is a critical success factor.

Looping in Externals

With every revolution, the organization not only learns what features are most useful for the users, but the project team also learns how to build enticing user experiences, how to speed up development cycles, or how to scale the system to meet increasing demand. This learning cycle is critical for the organization's digital transformation because it enables in-house innovation and rapid iterations.

Inversely, if corporate IT depends very much on the work of external providers, which is rather common, the ones benefiting from this learning are the external consultants. Organizations should therefore place their internal staff inside the learning cycle and use external support mainly to coach or teach them. Taking this logic a step further, digital transformation starts with transforming HR and recruiting practices to hire qualified staff and to educate existing employees so they can become part of the learning cycle.

Pivoting the Layer Cake

To speed up the feedback engine you need to turn the organizational layer cake on its side by forming teams that carry full responsibility from product concept to technical implementation, operations, and refinement. Often such an approach carries the label of "tribes", "feature teams", or "DevOps", which is associated with a "you build it, you run it" attitude. Doing so not only provides a direct feedback loop to the developers about the quality of their product (pagers going off in the middle of the night are a very immediate form of feedback), but it also *scales the organization* (26) by removing unnecessary synchronization points: all relevant decisions can be made within the project team.

Running in independent teams that focus on rapid feedback has one other fundamental advantage: it brings the customer back into the picture. In the traditional pyramid of layered command-and-control the customer is nowhere to be found - at best somewhere interacting with the lowest layer of the organization, far from where decisions are made and strategies are set. In contrast, "vertical" teams draw feedback and their energy directly from the customer.

The main challenge in assembling such teams is to get a complete range of skill sets into a compact team, ideally not exceeding the size of a "2 pizza team" that can be fed by 2 large pizzas. This requires qualified staff, a willingness to collaborate across skill sets, and a low-friction environment.

Maintaining Cohesion

If all control rests in the vertically integrated team, what ensures that these teams are still part of one company and for example use common branding and common infrastructure? It's OK to have some pie crust on the vertical layer cake, for example one at the top for branding and overall strategy and one at the bottom for common infrastructure that *never sends a human to do a machine's job* (14).

Once you have perfected the rapid Build - Measure - Learn feedback cycle you may wonder how many revolutions you have to make. In digital companies the feedback engine stops spinning only when the product is dead. That's why for once it's good to be part of an infinite loop.

33. You can't fake IT

Becoming Digital Inside-Out

Who can spot the dinosaur programmer?

Rapid feedback cycles (32) help digital companies understand customer demand and improve the product or service offered. Naturally, this feedback loop works best when the product or service has direct exposure to the end customer or consumer. Corporate IT, in contrast, is relatively far removed from the end customer because it supplies IT services to the business, which in turn is in contact with the customer. Does this imply that corporate IT shouldn't be the focal point for digital transformation as it's too far removed from the digital customers? Many digital transformation initiatives that are driven "from the top" appear to support this notion: they have special teams engage with customers in focus groups before handing down the specs to IT for implementation.

Laying the Foundation

But just like you cannot build a fancy new house on an old, fragile foundation, you cannot be digital on the outside without transforming the IT engine room: IT must deliver those capabilities to the business that are needed to become agile and to compete in the digital marketplace. If it takes eight weeks to procure a virtual server based on an e-mail request, the business cannot scale up with demand, unless it stockpiles a huge number of idling servers, which would be the exact opposite of what cloud computing promises. Worse yet, if these servers are setup with an old version of the operating system, modern applications may not be able to run on them. On top of all this, necessary manual network changes are guaranteed to break things or slow them down.

Feedback Cycles

Rapidly deploying servers can be solved with private cloud technologies, but that alone doesn't make IT "digital". For corporate IT to credibly offer services to the business competing in a digital world, it must itself be ready to compete in the digital world of IT service providers, not only from a cost and quality perspective, but also from an engagement model point-of-view: corporate IT must become customer-centric and learn from customers using its products in an *Infinite Loop* (32). If the servers that are provisioned aren't the ones the customer needs, then provisioning them faster accomplishes nothing. Moreover, the customer may not actually want to order servers at all, but prefers to deploy applications on a Platform-as-a-Service solution or one of the so-called "serverless" architectures. To understand these trends, IT must engage with their internal customers, the business units, in a rapid feedback loop, just like the business units do with their end customers.

Delivering On Your Promises

Engaging with customers is only helpful if you can deliver on their demands. In the case of IT delivering services to its customers, the business units, it must have the capability and the attitude to deliver digital services rapidly at high quality. An MIT study[103] showed that those companies that aligned business and IT without first improving their IT delivery capability actually spent *more* money on IT but suffered from below-average revenue growth. You can't fake being digital.

Customer Centricity

Customer centricity is a common phrase incorporated into many a company's motto or "value statement". Which company wouldn't want to be *customer centric*, after all? Even institutions whose customers are decreed by law, such as the Internal Revenue Service, have exhibited a good dose of customer awareness in recent years. For many organizations, though, it's difficult to move beyond the simple slogan and truly become customer-centric because it requires fundamental changes to the organizational culture and setup: hierarchical organizations are CEO-centered, not customer-centered. Operational teams following ITIL processes are process-centered, not customer-centered. IT run as a cost center is likely cost-centered as opposed to customer-centered. Running a customer-centric business on top of a process- or CEO-centric IT is bound to generate enormous friction.

Co-creating IT Services

To support a business in digital transformation, it's no longer enough for IT to develop commodity services that are pushed to the customers, i.e. the business units, via *Governance* (28). IT must start

---

[103]http://sloanreview.mit.edu/article/avoiding-the-alignment-trap-in-it/

to behave like a digital business, generating "pull" demand instead of pushing product. This can be done well by developing products jointly with customers, which goes under the fancy moniker of "co-creation". While many internal customers will welcome the change in mindset and the opportunity to influence a service being built, others may not want to engage unless you present a firm price and service-level agreement. Being digital only works if your customers are digital. In most cases, this isn't a problem because the market forces the business to become digital, which presents IT with a digital customer.

Eat Your Own Dog Food

 Google is famous for *dogfooding* its products, meaning its employees get to try alpha or beta versions of new products. While the name doesn't make it sound too appealing, Google's "food" includes pretty exciting products, some of which never reach the eyes of the consumer. It reminds me of an old friend of mine who determined that it's unfair that his dog eats dog food while he's having tasty dinner. He decided to share his meal with his dog instead (and the vet confirmed the dog is perfectly healthy doing this).

Dogfooding is effective because it enables an extremely rapid feedback and learning cycle in a safe and controlled environment. I start all my IT services by offering them first as an internal Beta Release. Once we better understand customer expectations and work out the kinks, we offer them to external customers.

Google took things a step further and merged employee and customer accounts into a single user management system, making customer and employees appear identical to most applications, differentiated only by their domain name (google.com) and their access from the corporate network. Merging the previously disparate systems was rather painful, but the effect was hugely liberating as employees were treated as customers.

In contrast, traditional organizations can look at employees and customers very differently.

At a large company, employees weren't supposed to use Android phones. While I didn't even debate the technical merit, I couldn't help but wonder how this company can then support customers using Android devices, which make up over 80% of the market. If Android isn't considered secure enough for employees, how can it be considered secure for a financial services organization's customers?

Rather than trying to control the user base, it'd be more helpful to understand and address potential weaknesses, for example through two-factor authentication, mobile device management, fraud monitoring, or disallowing old versions of the operating system, both for customers and employees.

Digital Mindset

Besides starting to use their own products and learning to iterate, one of the biggest hurdles in making corporate IT more digital can be the employees' mindset. When employees use previous-generation Blackberry phones and internal processes are handled by e-mailing spreadsheets based on rules documented in a slide deck, then it's difficult to believe that an organization can act digitally. While it's a touchy subject, the age distribution in traditional IT can be an additional challenge: the average age in corporate IT is often in the 40s or early 50s, far removed from the digital natives that are being courted as the new digital customer segment. Bringing younger employees into the mix can help towards becoming digital as it brings some of your target customer segment in-house.

The good news is that change can happen gradually, starting with small steps. When employees start using LinkedIn to pull photos or resumes instead of e-mailing resume templates, it's a step to becoming digital. Checking Google Maps to find convenient hotels instead of the clunky travel portal is another. Building small internal applications to automate approval processes is a small, but very important step: it gets people into a "maker mindset" that motivates them to tackle problems by building solutions, not by referring to outdated rule books. The digital feedback cycle can only work if people can build solutions. This may be the biggest hurdle for Corporate IT because it is too *afraid of code* (11). Code is what software innovation is made of, so if you want to be digital, you better learn to code!

Opportunities for making small steps towards becoming digital are plentiful. I tend to look for little problems to solve or small things to speed up and automate.

 At Google, getting a USB charger cable was a matter of 2.5 minutes: 1 minute to walk to the nearest *Tech Stop*, 30 seconds to swipe your badge and scan the cable at the self-checkout, and 1 minute to walk back to your desk. In corporate IT, I had to mail someone, who mailed someone, who asked me the type of phone I use and then entered an order, which I had to approve. Elapsed time: about 2 weeks. Speed factor: 14 days x 24 hours/day x 60 minutes/hour / 2.5 minutes = 8064, in the same league as *setting up a Source Code Repository* (31).

Fixing this would make a great mini-project. You don't see a positive business case? That's probably because your company isn't yet set up to develop solutions rapidly. A digital company could likely build this solution in an afternoon, including database and Web user interface, and host it in their private cloud basically for free. If you never start building small, rapid solutions, your IT will be paralyzed and likely unable to act in a digital environment.

The Stack Fallacy

As much of corporate IT is focused on infrastructure and operations, becoming *software-minded* (15) requires a huge shift. For example, my idea to build an *On Air Sign* (26) that illuminates when my IP desk phone is *off hook* never materialized because the team rolling out the devices didn't code or deal with software APIs.

The challenge an organization faces when "moving up the stack", e.g. from infrastructure to application software platform or from software platform to end-user application is well-known and has aptly been labeled as the Stack fallacy[104]. Even successful companies underestimate the challenge and are subject to the fallacy: VMware missed the shift from virtualization software to Docker containers, Cisco has been spending Billions in acquisitions to get closer to application delivery, and even mighty Google failed to move from utility software like search and mail to an engaging social network, a market dominated by FaceBook.

For most of corporate IT this means an uphill climb from a focus on operating infrastructure to engaging users with rapidly evolving applications and services. While challenging, it's doable: internal IT doesn't have to compete in the open market, giving it the chance to change in small increments. Ultimately, actively funding this change will see a significant return from a truly digital IT organization.

---

[104]http://techcrunch.com/2016/01/18/why-big-companies-keep-failing-the-stack-fallacy/

34. Money can't buy Love

Nor a culture change

I need that feature by Tuesday

After transitioning from a Silicon Valley company to a traditional business, my new coworkers frequently reminded me that we're a large corporation, implying that what works for Google wouldn't apply here. My routine retort was that by applying the standard measure of market capitalization, I joined a corporation 10 times smaller. More interestingly, my coworkers also pointed out that Google can do pretty much do whatever they want thanks to all the money they have. My view, in contrast, was that many successful traditional businesses suffer exactly from having too much money.

Innovator's Dilemma

How can organizations have too much money? After all, their goal is to maximize profits and shareholders returns. To do so, companies use stringent budgeting processes that control spending. For example, proposed projects are assessed by their expected rate of return against a benchmark typically set by existing investments, sometimes called IRR, "Internal Rate of Return".

Such processes can hurt innovation, though, when new ideas have to compete with existing, highly profitable "cash cows". Most innovative products can't match established products' performance or profitability during early stages. Traditional budgeting processes may therefore reject new and promising ideas, a phenomenon that Christensen coined the *Innovator's Dilemma*[105]. However, when they later surpass sustaining technologies, they threaten organizations that didn't invest early on and now lag behind.

Rich companies tend to have a high IRR and are therefore especially likely to reject new ideas. Also, they perceive the risk of no change as low – after all, things are going great. This dampens the appetite for change (see *No Pain, No Change* (29)) and increases the danger of disruption.

Beware of the HPPO

Despite its downsides, companies making investment decisions based on expected return at least use a consistent decision metric. Many rich companies have a different decision process: that of *HPPO*, the *Highest Paid Person's Opinion*. This approach isn't just highly subjective but also susceptible to shiny, HPPO-targeted vendor demos, which peddle incremental "enterprise" solutions as opposed to real innovation. Because those decision makers are far removed from actual technology and software delivery, they don't realize how fast new solutions can be built on a shoestring budget.

---

[105]Christensen: The Innovator's Dilemma, Harper Business; Reprint edition, 2011

To make matters worse, internal "sales people" exploit management's limited understanding to push their own pet projects, often at a cost orders of magnitude higher than what digital companies would spend. I have seen someone make it to board level with the idea of exposing functionality as an API, at a cost of many million Euros. It's easy to sell people in the stone age a wheel.

Overhead and Tolerated Inefficiency

Many established companies with a profitable business model carry significant overhead: fancy corporate offices, old labor contracts with extremely generous retirement provisions, overemployment for roles that are no longer needed, an army of administrative staff for executives, company cars, drivers, car washes, private dining rooms, coffee and cake being served in board rooms – the list is long. This overhead cost is generally distributed across all cost centers, placing an enormous financial burden on small and innovative teams working on disruptive technologies.

My small team of architects was loaded with overhead cost ranging from office space and cafeteria subsidies to workplace charges (computers, phones), which I couldn't influence. In comparison, free meals offered by digital companies are a trivial expense.

Overhead costs also result from inefficiencies that are tolerated in wealthy organizations because there's little pressure to remove them. Examples are manifold: labor-intensive manual processes (I have seen people manually preparing spreadsheets from SAP data every month), lengthy meetings with 20 executives, half of whom have little to contribute, ordering processes with long paper trails, people printing reams of paper as handouts for meetings on digital strategy. All these line items add up and make it difficult for large companies to compete in new segments where margins aren't yet rich enough to support such overhead.

Hollowed-out IT

A particularly dangerous pitfall for wealthy organizations looking to transform is the belief that any required skill can be bought at will.

 In the late 1990s, the telecom business was very profitable thanks to a fast-growing broadband Internet market. These companies outsourced virtually all technical work to external contractors and system integrators (where I was employed). Solid profits allowed them to digest the high consulting fees, high administrative overhead for contract management, and more than occasional project cost overruns.

These companies considered IT a commodity: necessary, but not a competitive advantage. That's why they didn't perceive any risk in keeping IT skills outside of the company. Instead, they valued the flexibility to ramp external IT staff up and down as needed just like they would do with administrative or cleaning staff.

However, this model has severe drawbacks in the digital age: first, it prevents the organization from effectively participating in the *Build-Measure-Learn Cycle* (32) because externals typically work on a pre-negotiated scope-of-work and therefore have little incentive to keep iterating on products or to shorten release cycles. Second, the organization won't be able to develop a deep understanding of new technologies and their potential, thus stifling innovation. Worse yet, in many cases even knowledge of the existing system landscape rests with external contractors, rendering the organization unable to make rational decisions based on the status quo. If you don't know your starting point, it's difficult to get on the road to change.

These companies' IT departments degenerated into mere budget administration structures with hardly any technology skill. The main skill needed was securing budget and spending it. Those companies couldn't attract much real IT talent because qualified candidates realized that their skills weren't valued. Nevertheless, all was perceived as working well while the money flowed freely.

External Dependencies

But then change happened, with dramatic effects: hardly any industry was overrun by the digital companies as spectacularly as telecommunications. Telecoms used to "own" communication but completely failed to see the potential of the smart phone and digital consumer services. Existing IT contracts focused on *improving efficiency* (31) in back-end processing, such as billing; no internal skill was available to design and deliver new services to customers; and existing organizational structures and processes squashed any innovation that was trying to happen.

Eventually, telecoms were left with providing "dumb data pipes" in a downward price spiral while digital companies enjoyed almost-Trillion-Dollar valuations and rich profit margins. Experienced software architects know that too many external dependencies get you in trouble. The same is true for organizations.

Paying More May Get You Less

Other factors surely played a role in telecoms missing the "digital boat", but believing that technology skills can be acquired as needed is particularly dangerous. Just like you cannot buy friends, a company cannot buy motivated employees. Candidates with highly marketable skill sets, such as cloud architectures or machine learning, are attracted to teams with strong, like-minded people. This presents traditional companies with a chicken-and-egg problem.

Many companies try to overcome this hurdle by paying higher salaries. However, compensation is often not the main motivator for top candidates – they are looking for an employer where they can learn from their peers and implement projects rapidly to demonstrate impact. That's why it's difficult for companies to "buy" skilled employees. Worse yet, trying to attract talent by offering higher salaries can backfire: first, it'll attract "mercenary" developers who work for the money alone. Second, my experience is that people who come for money leave for more money. It won't attract passionate developers who want to be part of a high-performing team to change the world. I compare this pitfall to the unpopular kid handing out candy at school: the kid won't make friends, but will be surrounded by children who are willing to pretend to be a friend in exchange for candy.

Changing Culture from Within

Top consultants can surely help you implement new and exciting technology projects, but they won't significantly change the organization's culture - the cultural change has to come from within. Roberts[106] classifies the describing characteristics of an organization as PARC – people, architecture (structures), routines (processes), and culture. Restructurings and process reengineering can change the organization's architecture and routines, but cultural changes must be instilled by the company leadership. This takes time, lots of energy, and sometimes a leadership change: "to do change management, sometimes you have to change management." Because digital transformation requires changing both technology and culture, I opted to drive a large-scale IT transformation from the inside. It's the hard, but the only sustainable way.

---

[106]Roberts: The Modern Firm: Organizational Design for Performance and Growth, Oxford University Press, 2007

35. Who Likes Standing in Line?

Good Things Don't Come to Those Who Wait

100% Utilization

When in university, we often wonder whether and how what we learn will help us in our future careers and lives. While I am still waiting for the Ackerman function to accelerate my professional advancement (our first semester in computer science blessed us with a lecture on computability), the class on queuing theory was actually helpful: not only can you talk to the people in front of you in the supermarket checkout line about M/M/1 systems and the benefits of *single queue, multiple servers* systems (which most supermarkets don't use), but it also gives you an important foundation to reason about *Economies of Speed* (31).

Looking Between the Activities

When looking to speed things up in enterprises, most people look at how work is done: are all machines and people utilized, are they working efficiently? Ironically, when looking for speed, you mustn't look at the activities, but *between* them. By looking at activities you may find inefficient activity, but between the activities is where you find *inactivity*, things sitting around and waiting to be worked on. Inactivity can have a much more detrimental effect on speed than inefficient activity. If a machine is working well and almost 100% utilized, but a widget has to wait 3 months to be processed by that machine, you may have replicated the public health care system, which is guided by efficiency, but certainly not speed. Many statistics show that typical processes in corporate IT, such as ordering a server, consist to over 90% of wait times. Instead of working more we should wait less!

A Little Bit of Queuing Theory

When you look between activities, you are bound to find *queues*, just like the lines at the doctor's or city office. To better understand how they work and what they do to a system, let's indulge in a bit of queuing theory. Our university textbook on queuing theory, Kleinrock's *Queuing Systems*[107], is still available, albeit a bit pricey. But don't worry, you don't need to digest 400 pages of queuing theory to understand enterprise transformation.

Our university professor reminded us that if we remember only one thing from his class, it should be *Little's Result*. This equation states that in a stable system, the total processing time T, which includes wait time, is equal to N, the number of items in the system

---

[107]Leonard Kleinrock: Queueing Systems. Volume 1: Theory, Wiley-Interscience, 1975

(the ones in the queue plus the ones being processed) divided by the processing rate λ, in short $T = N/\lambda$. This makes intuitive sense: the longer the queue, the longer it takes for new items to be processed. If you are processing 2 items per second and there are 10 items on average in the systems, a newly arriving item will spend 5 seconds in the system. You might already guess that most of those 5 seconds are spent in the queue, not actually processing the item. The noteworthy aspect of Little's result is that the relationship holds for most arrival and departure distributions.

To build a bridge between speed and efficiency, we need to look at the relationship between utilization and wait time. The system is utilized whenever an item is being processed, meaning one or more items are in the system. If you sum up the probability that a given number of items are in the system, i.e. 0 items (the system is idle), 1 (one item being processed), 2 (one item being processed plus one in the queue), etc., you find that the average number of items in the system is equal to $\rho / (1 - \rho)$ where ρ designates the *utilization rate*, or the fraction of time the server is busy (we make the assumption that arrivals are independent, which is described as a *memoryless* system). From the equation you can quickly gather that high levels of utilization (ρ moving closer to 100%) lead to extreme queue sizes and therefore wait times. Increasing utilization from 60% to 80% almost triples the average queue length: $0.6/(1 - 0.6) = 1.5$ vs. $0.8/(1 - 0.8) = 4$. Driving up utilization will drive away your customers because they get tired of standing in line!

Finding Queues

Queuing theory proves that driving up utilization increases processing times: if you live in a world where speed counts, you have to stop chasing efficiency. Instead, you have to have a look at your queues. Sometimes these queues are visible like the lines at government offices where you take a number and wonder whether you'll be served before closing time. In corporate IT the queues are

generally less visible – that's why so little attention is paid to them.
By looking a little harder, you can find a them almost everywhere,
though:

- *Busy calendars*: When everyone's calendar is 90% "utilized",
  topics queue for people to meet and discuss. I waited for
  meetings with senior executives for multiple months.
- *Steering meetings*: Such regular meetings tend to occur once
  a month or every quarter. Topics will be queued up for them,
  often holding up decisions or project progress.
- *E-mail*: Inboxes fill up with items that would take you a mere
  3 minutes to take care of, but that you don't get to for several
  days because you are highly "utilized" in meetings all day.
  Stuff often rots in my inbox queue for weeks.
- *Software releases*: Code that is written and tested but waiting
  for a release is sitting in a queue, sometimes for 6 months.
- *Workflow*: Many processes for anything from getting an in-
  voice paid to requesting a raise for employees have excessive
  wait times built in. For example, ordering a book takes large
  companies multiple weeks, as opposed to having it delivered
  the next day from Amazon.

To get a feeling for the damage done by queues, consider that
ordering a server often takes 4 weeks or more. The infrastructure
team won't actually bend metal to build a brand new server just
for you: most servers are provisioned as virtual machines these
days (thanks to *Software Eating the World* (15)). If you reasonably
assume that there are 4 hours of actual work in setting up a server
consisting of assigning an IP address, loading an operating system
image, doing some non-automated installations and configurations,
the time spent in the queue makes up 99.4% of the total time! That's
why we should look at the queues. Reducing the 4 hours of effort
to 2 won't make any difference unless you reduce the wait times.

Cutting the Line

Standing in line is hardly productive, but occasionally entertaining. When waiting in line at the San Francisco Marina post office I observed the highly utilized and actually quite friendly postal workers. To give myself a bit of utilization I stepped over to grab Priority Mail envelopes for my next urgent mailing (back then I didn't know what cool things[108] the Graffiti Research Lab guys made from postal supplies). When returning to my spot in the line the guy behind me complained and after a brief argument he claimed: "You are out of line." I think the irony of his statement escaped him as I was the only one who was amused.

 Digital companies understand the danger of queues quite well. The infamously tasty and free Google cafés have signs posted stating that: "cutting the line is encouraged." Google doesn't like to bear the opportunity cost of 20 people politely waiting behind a person who transports salad leaves to their plate one-by-one.

Making Queues Visible

"You can't manage what you can't measure" goes the old saying, apparently falsely attributed to Edwards Deming. In the case of queues, making them visible can be a major step towards managing them. For example, metrics extracted from the ticketing system can show the time spent in each step or the ratio of effort over elapsed time (you will be shocked!) Showing that most time is simply spent waiting could also help the organization *Think in New Dimensions* (36), e.g. to realize that more elapsed time doesn't equate to higher quality.

---

[108]https://www.flickr.com/groups/graffitiresearchlab/pool/tags/postalchairs/

For critical business processes, such as insurance claims handling, queue metrics are often managed under the umbrella of Business Activity Monitoring (BAM). Corporate IT should use BAM to measure its own business, such as provisioning software and hardware, and reduce lag times. Slow IT these days means slow business.

Why are *single queue, multiple server* systems more efficient and why don't supermarkets use them? Lining customers up in a single queue reduces the chances that a server (i.e. cashier) is idling due to an uneven distribution of customers across the queues. It also allows smooth increases or reduction in the number of cashiers without everyone running to the newly opened lane or being ticked off at a lane closing. Most importantly, it eliminates the frustration that the other line is always moving faster! However, a single queue requires a bit more floor space and a single entry point for customers. You will see the *single queue, multiple server* in many post offices and some large electronic stores like Fry's Electronics.

Postscript: Message Queues

How can the co-author of a book on asynchronous message queues[109] conclude that queues are trouble? Queues are a great tool for building high throughput and resilient systems. They buffer load spikes to allow resources to work at optimum rates. Just imagine each person who wants to check out of the supermarket just piling their items onto the checkout counter the moment they reach. Hardly a useful scenario. Many businesses, such as Starbucks use queues (see *Your Coffee Shop Does Not Use 2-Phase Commit* (8)) to optimize throughput.

Queues become troublesome when they get long due to excessive utilization rates. High utilization and short response times don't mix. Don't blame the queue for it.

---

[109]Hohpe, Woolf: Enterprise Integration Patterns, Addison-Wesley, 2003

36. Thinking in Four Dimensions

More degrees of freedom can make your head hurt

Stuck in two dimensions

Our university class on coding theory taught us about spheres in an n-dimensional space. While the math behind it made a good bit of sense (the spheres represent the "error radius" for encoding while the space between the sphere is "waste" in the coding scheme), trying to visualize four-dimensional spheres can make your head hurt a good bit. However, thinking in more dimensions can be the key to transforming the way you think about your IT and your business.

Living Along a Line

IT architecture is a profession of trade-offs: flexibility brings complexity, decoupling increases latency, distributing components introduces communication overhead. The architect's role is often to determine the "best" spot on such a continuum, based on experience and an understanding of the system context and requirements. A system's architecture is essentially defined by the combination of trade-offs made across multiple continua.

Quality vs. Speed

When looking at development methods, one well-known trade-off is between quality and speed: if you have more time, you can achieve better quality because you have time to build things properly and to test more extensively to eliminate remaining defects. If you count how many times you have heard the argument: "we would like to have a better (more reusable, scalable, standardized) architecture, but we just don't have time", you start to believe that this god-given trade-off is taught in the first lecture of "IT project management 101". The ubiquitous slogan "quick-and-dirty" further underlines this belief.

The folks bringing this argument often also like to portray companies or teams that are moving fast as undisciplined "cowboys" or as building software where quality doesn't matter as much as in their "serious" business, because they cannot distinguish *Fast Discipline from Slow Chaos* (27). The term *banana product* is sometimes used in this context – a product that supposedly ripens in the hands of the customer. Again, speed is equated with a disregard for quality.

Ironically, the cause for the "we don't have time" argument is often self-initiated as the project teams tend to spend many months documenting and reviewing requirements or getting approval, until finally upper management puts their fist on the table and demands some progress. During all these preparation phases the team "forgot" to talk to the architecture team until someone in budgeting catches them and sends them over for an architecture review which invariably begins with "I'd love to do it better, but..." The consequence is a fragmented IT landscape consisting of a haphazard collection of ad-hoc decisions because there was never enough time to "do it right" and no business case to fix it later. The old saying "nothing lasts as long as the temporary solution" certainly holds in corporate IT. Most of these solutions last until the software they are built on is going out of vendor support and becomes a security risk.

More Degrees of Freedom

So what if we add a dimension to the seemingly linear trade-off between quality and speed? Luckily, we are only moving from one to two dimensions, so our head shouldn't hurt as much as with the n-dimensional spheres. We'd simply have to plot speed and quality on two separate axes of a coordinate system instead of on a single line. Now we can portray the trade-off between the two parameters as a curve whose shape depicts how much speed we have to give up to achieve how much better quality.

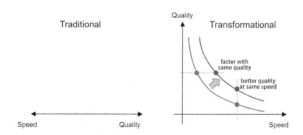

Moving from one to two dimensions.

For simplicity's sake, you could assume the relationship is linear, depicted by a straight line. This probably isn't quite true, though: as we aim to approach zero defects, the time we need to spend in testing probably goes up a lot and as we know, testing can only prove the presence of defects, but not the absence. Developing software for life- and safety-critical systems or things that are shot into space are probably positioned on this end of the spectrum, and rightly so. That they rarely achieve zero defects can be seen by the example of the mars climate orbiter, which disintegrated due to a unit error between metric and US measures. At the other end of the continuum, in the "now or never zone", you may simply reach the limits of how fast you can go. You'd have to slow down a good bit and spend at least some time on proper design and testing to improve quality. So the relationship likely looks more like a concave curve which asymptotically approaches the extremes at the two axes.

The trade-off between time (speed) and quality still holds in this 2-dimensional view, but you can reason much more rationally about the relationship between the two. This is a classic example of how even a *simple model can sharpen your thinking* (6).

Changing the Rules of the Game

Once you moved into the two-dimensional space, you can ask a much more profound question: "can we shift the curve?" And: "if so, what would it take to shift it?" Shifting the curve to the upper right would give you better quality at the same speed or faster speed without sacrificing quality. Changing the shape or position of the curve means we no longer have to move along a fixed continuum between speed and quality. Heresy? Or a doorstep to a hidden world of productivity?

Probably both, but that's exactly what digital companies have achieved: they have shifted the curve significantly to achieve never-before-seen speeds in IT delivery while maintaining feature quality and system stability. How do they do it? A big factor is following processes that are *optimized for speed* (31), as opposed to resource utilization or schedule predictability. The key ingredients are of technical or architectural nature: automation, independent deployability of code modules, resilient run-times, advanced monitoring, analytics, etc:

- They understand that software runs fast and predictably, so they *never send a human to do a machine's job* (14).
- They turn as many problems as possible into software problems, so they can automate them and hence move faster and often more predictably.
- If something does go wrong, they can react quickly, often with the users barely noticing. This is possible because everything is automated and they *use Version Control* (15).
- They build resilient systems, ones that can absorb disturbance and self-heal, instead of trying to predict and eliminate all failure scenarios.

Inverting the Curve

If adding a new dimension doesn't make folks' head hurt enough, tell them that in software development it's even possible to invert the curve: faster software often means better software! Much time in software development is spent due to friction and manual tasks: long wait times for severs or environments to be set up, manual regressing testing, etc. Removing this friction, usually by *Automating Everything* (14), not only speeds up software development but also increases quality because manual tasks are a common source of errors. As a result, you can use speed as a lever to *increase* quality.

What Quality?

When speaking about speed and quality, one should take a moment to consider what quality really means. Most traditional IT folks would define it as the software's conformance to specification and possibly adherence to a schedule. System uptime and reliability are surely also part of quality. These facets of quality have the essence of *predictability*: we got what we asked or wished for at the time we were promised it. But how do we know whether we asked for the right thing? Probably someone asked the users, so the requirements reflect what they wanted the system to do. But do they know what they really want, especially if you are building a system the users have never seen before? One of Kent Beck's great sayings is: "I want to build a system the users *wish* they asked for."

The traditional definition of quality is a *proxy metric*: we presuppose to know what the customers want, or at least that they know what they want. What if this proxy isn't a very reliable indicator? Companies living in the digital world don't pretend to know exactly what their customers want because they are building brand-new solutions. Instead of asking their customers what they want, *they observe customer behavior* (32). Based on the observed behavior they quickly adjust and improve their product, often trying out new things using A/B testing. One could argue that this results in a product of much higher quality, one that the customers wish they could have asked for. So one cannot only shift the curve of how much quality you can get for how much speed, you can also change what quality you are aiming for. Maybe this is yet another dimension?

Losing a Dimension

What happens when a person who is used to working in a world with more degrees of freedom enters a world with fewer? This can lead to a lot of surprises and some headaches, almost like moving from our three-dimensional world to the Planiverse[110]. The best way out is education and *Leading Change* (30).

---

[110]https://en.wikipedia.org/wiki/The_Planiverse

Architecting IT Transformation

Transforming from Bottom-up

This book's main purpose is to encourage IT architects to take an active role in transforming traditional IT organizations who must compete with digital disruptors. "Why are technical architects supposed to take on this enormous task?", you may ask, and rightly so: many managers or IT leaders may have strong communication and leadership abilities that are needed to change organizations. However, today's digital revolution is not just any organizational restructuring, but one that is driven by IT innovation: mobile devices, cloud computing, data analytics, wireless networking, and the Internet of Things, to name a few.

Leading an organization into the digital future therefore necessitates a thorough understanding of the underlying technologies along with their application for competitive advantage. It's hard to imagine that instigating a digital transformation purely from "the top down" can be successful. Non-tech-savvy management can at best limp along based on input from external consultants or trade journals. That's not going to cut it, though: competition in the digital world is fierce and customer expectations are increasing every day. When we hear of a successful start-up company that went public or was acquired for a huge sum of money, we usually forget the dozens or even hundreds of start-ups in the same space that didn't make it despite a great idea and a bunch of smart people working extremely hard on it. Architects, who are rooted in technology, are needed to help drive the transformation.

If you are not yet convinced that transforming the organization is part of your job as an architect, you may not have much of a choice: recent technology advances can only be successfully implemented if the organizational structure, processes, and often the culture also change. For example, "DevOps" style development is enabled through the advent of automation technologies, but relies on breaking down *change* and *run* silos. Cloud computing can reduce time-to-market and IT cost dramatically, but only if the organization and its processes empower developers to actually provision servers and make necessary network changes. Lastly, being successful with data analytics requires the organization to stop making decisions based on management slide sets, but on hard data. All these are major organizational transformations. Technology evolution has become inseparable from organizational evolution. Correspondingly, the job of the architect has broadened from designing new IT systems to also designing a matching organization and culture.

Transforming from Inside-out

Most digital markets are winner-takes-all markets: Google owns search, FaceBook owns social, Amazon owns fulfillment and cloud, Netflix mostly owns content (battling with Amazon). Apple and Google's Android own mobile. Google tried to get into social and floundered. Microsoft struggles in search and mobile. Amazon also struggles in mobile just like Google repeatedly dabbles in fulfillment and can never quite get traction. In cloud computing even almighty Google is at best a runner-up with Amazon holding a huge lead. Watching this battle of the titans from the sidelines of a traditional organization often resembles watching world-class athletes compete from the bleachers while eating popcorn: these organizations sport multi-hundred-Billion Dollar evaluations (Netflix being the "baby" with roughly $50B market capitalization in 2016), have access to world's top IT talent, and are run by extremely talented and skilled management teams.

Watching vendor demos and purchasing a few new products aren't going to make an organization competitive against these guys. As the overall direction of the digital revolution has become fairly clear, and technology has been democratized to the point where every individual with a credit card can procure servers and big data analytics engines within minutes, the main competitive asset for an organization is its ability to learn fast. External consultants and vendors can give a boost, but cannot substitute for *an organization's ability to learn* (32). Architects are therefore needed to drive or at least support the transformation from inside the organization.

From Ivory Tower Resident to Corporate Savior

In times of digital disruption, the job of the IT architect has become more challenging: keeping pace with ever faster technology evolution, but also being well-versed in organizational engineering, understanding corporate strategy, and communicating to upper management is now part of being an architect. But the architect's job has also become more meaningful and rewarding, if he or she takes up the challenge. The new world does not reward architects who draw diagrams while sitting in the ivory tower, but hands-on innovation drivers and change agents. I hope this book encourages you to take the challenge and equips you with useful guidance and a little wisdom along your way.

37. All I Have to Offer Is the Truth

Giving Folks the Red Pill

It's so much more comfortable up here

Embarking on a transformation journey can be quite a dramatic, sometimes even traumatic, undertaking for many people working for traditional enterprises. Digital companies are run, or at least perceived to be run, by highly educated, 20-something "digital natives", who aren't distracted by family or social life and require little to no sleep. Their employers have hardly any legacy to deal with and Billions in the bank, despite offering most services to consumers for free. For IT staff who has been working in the same, traditional enterprise, following the same processes for decades, this is likely to cause a mix of fear, denial, and resentment.

Getting these folks on board for a transformation agenda is thus a delicate affair: if you are too gentle, people may not see a need to change. If you are too direct, people may panic or resent you.

Nothing but the truth

Extorting a final reference from the movie *The Matrix*, when Morpheus asks Neo to choose between the red pill, which will eject him into reality, and the blue pill, which will keep him inside the illusion of the Matrix, he doesn't describe what "reality" looks like. Morpheus merely states:

> Remember: all I'm offering is the truth. Nothing more.

If he had told Neo that the truth translates into living in the confines of a bare bones hovercraft ship patrolling sewers in the middle of a war against the machines who perpetually hunt the ship to chop it up with their powerful laser beams, he may have taken the blue pill. But Neo had already understood that there's something wrong with the current state, the Matrix illusion, and felt a strong desire to change the system. Most corporate IT residents, in contrast, are quite content with their current environment and position. So you likely need to push them a little harder to take the red pill.

Just like in the movie *The Matrix*, though, the new digital reality that awaits the red-pill-taking folks may not be exactly what they expected. In a meeting, a fellow architect once proudly proclaimed that for transformation to succeed the architect's life needs to be made easier. Aiming to make one's life easier is unlikely to lead into the digital future but will rather end up in disappointment. Technological advances and new ways of working make IT more interesting and valuable to the business, but they don't make it easier: new technologies have to be learned and the environment generally becomes more complex, all the while the pace picks up. Digital transformation isn't a matter of convenience, but of corporate survival.

Digital Paradise?

Looking from the outside, working at digital companies appears to largely consist of free lunches, massages, and riding Segways. While digital companies do court their employees with an unheard-of list of perks, they are also hugely competitive internally and externally. They firmly embrace a culture of constant change and speed to remain competitive and drive innovation. This means that employees rarely get to rest on the laurels of their work, but have to keep pushing on. Engineers don't join digital companies to relax, but to push the envelope, innovate, and change the world.

The rewards match the challenge, though, not just financially, but most importantly in enabling engineers to really make a difference and accomplish things they wouldn't be able to accomplish on their own. Over a decade ago at Google you could scale an application you wrote to 100,000 servers and run analytics against Petabytes of logs in a second or two. Most traditional companies still dream of these capabilities a decade later. Such are the rewards of the digital IT life. These examples also show traditional companies why they should be scared.

Half of Heaven can be Hell

When looking to transform, traditional companies often identify practices employed by digital disruptors and try to import them into their traditional way of working. While it's important to understand how your competitors think and work, adopting their practices requires careful consideration. Digital companies are known to do things like storing all their source code in a single repository, not having any architects, or letting employees work on whatever they like. When admiring these techniques, traditional companies must realize that they are watching world-class superstars pulling off amazing stunts. Yes, there are people who walk a tightrope between skyscrapers or jump off a tower to glide into the rooftop pool of a nearby building. This doesn't mean you should try the same at home.

When adopting "digital" practices, an organization must understand the interdependencies between the practices. A single code repository requires a world-class build system that can scale to thousands of machines and execute incremental build and test cycles. Sticking all your code into a single repo without having such a system in place, and a team to maintain it, is like jumping off a building without a parachute. It's unlikely you'll be landing softly in the nearby rooftop pool.

Abandon Ship

For most organizations, sailing to the digital future is a matter of survival. Imagine you are an officer on the Titanic ocean liner and were just informed that the ship will be slowly, but surely sinking. Most of the passengers have no idea of the severity of the situation and are comfortably sipping Champagne on the upper decks. If you walk up to the passengers and individually inform them:

> Sir, excuse me if you wouldn't mind. Could you be so kind to consider relocating to the main deck so we may transfer you to a safer vessel? After you finish your drink, obviously. Please kindly excuse the terrible inconvenience. Your wellbeing is our primary concern.

You may not get much of a response, maybe just a doubtful stare. People may order another Champagne and then have a peek at the vessel you are suggesting, the lifeboat, just to conclude that it appears much less safe and convenient than staying on the world's most modern and unsinkable ocean liner.

On the other hand if, you inform the passengers as follows:

> This ship is sinking! Most of you will drown in the icy ocean because there aren't enough lifeboats.

you will cause widespread panic and a rush for the lifeboats that's likely to leave many passengers dead or injured even before the ship takes on water. Motivating corporate IT staff to start changing the way they work, and to leave behind the comfort of their current position is not dissimilar. They are also unlikely to realize their ship is sinking. Where on the spectrum of communication methods you should communicate depends on each organization and individual. I tend to start gentle and "ratchet up" the rhetoric when I observe inaction.

Looks are Deceiving

Just as it seems unlikely that a simple block of ice can sink a modern (at the time) marvel of engineering, small, digital companies may not feel threatening to a traditional enterprise. Most start-ups are run by relatively inexperienced, sometimes even naive people who believe they can revolutionize an industry while sitting on a beanbag because their office space hasn't been fully set up yet. They are often understaffed and have to secure multiple rounds of external funding before turning profitable, if ever at all.

However, just like 90% of an iceberg's volume lies under water, digital companies' enormous strength is hidden: it lies in their ability to learn much faster, often orders of magnitude faster than traditional organizations. Dismissing or trivializing start-ups' initial attempts to enter an established market could therefore be a fatal mistake. "They don't understand our business" is a common observation from traditional businesses. However, what took a business 50 years to learn may take a disruptor only 1 year or less because they are set up for *Economies of Speed* (31) and have amazing technology at their disposal.

Digital disruptors also don't have to *unlearn* bad habits. Learning new things is difficult, but unlearning existing processes, thought patterns, and assumptions is disproportionately more difficult. Unlearning and abandoning what made them successful in the past is one of the biggest transformation hurdles for traditional companies.

Some traditional businesses may feel safe from disruption because their industry is regulated. To demonstrate how thin a safety net regulation provides, I routinely remind business leaders that if the *digitals* have managed to put electric and self-driving cars on the road and rockets into space, they are surely capable of obtaining a banking or insurance license. For example, they could simply acquire a licensed company.

Lastly, digital disruptors don't tend to attack from the front. They tend to choose weak spots in existing business models that are highly inefficient, but not significant enough for large, traditional enterprises to pay attention to. AirBnB didn't build a better hotel and Fintech companies aren't interested in rebuilding a complete bank or insurance company. Rather, they attack the distribution channels, where inefficiency, high commissions, and unhappy customers allow new business models to scale rapidly with minimum capital investment. Some researchers claim that had the Titanic hit the iceberg head on, it might not have sunk. Instead, it was taken down because the iceberg tore open a large portion of the relatively weak side of the hull. That's where the digitals hit.

Distress Signals

While transformation can be a scary endeavor, you aren't the only architect who is accepting the challenge. Just like ships in distress, it's good to call for help when things look dire! You shouldn't be shy about sending a digital SOS – no one has a proven recipe for transformation, so exchanging experiences and anecdotes is mutually beneficial. You may even opt to share your experiences in a book. I'll be one of your first readers.

Printed in Great Britain
by Amazon

61207507R00180